PRAISE FOR KATE ZAMBRENO

"Kate Zambreno has invented a new form. It is a kind of absolute present, real life captured in closeup."
—**Annie Ernaux, Nobel Laureate in Literature**

"*Drifts* gathers up multiple ways of seeing, feeling and understanding, layering fiction, meditation, biography, confession and prose poetry into one capacious structure. This is an extraordinary book."
—**Margo Jefferson, author of *Negroland***

"A spirited, shape-shifting read that is by turns insightful, intimate, speculative, and mischievous. In their search to uncover the form's rich potential, Zambreno is unafraid to show us what they too are made of."
—**Claire-Louise Bennett, author of *Pond***

"*The Light Room* is a marvelous and marvel-filled book. Zambreno's mind is like a magic filter discovering secrets when turned on any sort of item—a tiny toy, a loom, an artist, a mortality. A wonderful book, a companion for all the varieties of days."
—**Rivka Galchen, author of *Little Labors***

"Thrillingly digressive lectures."
—**Leslie Jamison,** *The New York Times*

ANIMAL STORIES

KATE ZAMBRENO

**SCRIBNER
EDITIONS**

London · New York · Amsterdam/Antwerp · Sydney/Melbourne · Toronto · New Delhi

First published in the United States by Transit Books, 2025

First published in Great Britain by Scribner Editions,
an imprint of Simon & Schuster UK Ltd, 2026

Copyright © Kate Zambreno, 2025

SCRIBNER and design are registered trademarks of The Gale Group, Inc.,
used under licence by Simon & Schuster Inc.

The right of Kate Zambreno to be identified as author of this work has been
asserted in accordance with the Copyright, Designs and Patents Act, 1988.

1 3 5 7 9 10 8 6 4 2

Simon & Schuster UK Ltd, 1st Floor,
222 Gray's Inn Road, London WC1X 8HB

For more than 100 years, Simon & Schuster has championed authors and
the stories they create. By respecting the copyright of an author's intellectual
property, you enable Simon & Schuster and the author to continue publishing
exceptional books for years to come. We thank you for supporting the author's
copyright by purchasing an authorized edition of this book.
No amount of this book may be reproduced or stored in any format, nor may it be
uploaded to any website, database, language-learning model, or other repository,
retrieval, or artificial intelligence system without express permission. All rights
reserved. Inquiries may be directed to Simon & Schuster, 222 Gray's Inn Road,
London WC1X 8HB or RightsMailbox@simonandschuster.co.uk

Simon & Schuster Australia, Sydney
Simon & Schuster India, New Delhi

www.simonandschuster.co.uk
www.simonandschuster.com.au
www.simonandschuster.co.in

The authorised representative in the EEA is Simon & Schuster Netherlands BV,
Herculesplein 96, 3584 AA Utrecht, Netherlands. info@simonandschuster.nl

Simon & Schuster strongly believes in freedom of expression and stands against
censorship in all its forms. For more information, visit BooksBelong.com.

A CIP catalogue record for this book is available from the British Library

Trade Paperback ISBN: 978-1-3985-5623-2
eBook ISBN: 978-1-3985-5624-9

*The author and publishers have made all reasonable efforts to contact copyright-
holders for permission, and apologise for any omissions or errors in the form of
credits given. Corrections may be made to future printings.*

Printed and Bound in the UK using 100% Renewable Electricity
at CPI Group (UK) Ltd

for L & R

"It was around the same time that I started noticing the other animals."

DAISY HILDYARD, *The Second Body*

ZOO

STUDIES

MONKEY HOUSE

The Jardin des Plantes in Paris, which contains one of the world's oldest zoos, is located across the street from the Austerlitz train station. During the French Revolution, the king's royal zoo was pillaged at Versailles, and his collection of animals was mostly either eaten or destroyed. The animals that remained, including a lion and a rhinoceros, were spared a death sentence after the king was guillotined, and thus formed the beginnings of the first menagerie at the Jardin des Plantes: an abandoned royal collection joined by trained monkeys and dancing bears after the government seizure of circus animals in Paris, their former owners hired as the first zookeepers. Napoleon stocked the menagerie with a Noah's ark of animals. Crowds gathered to see an elephant, a zebra, a giraffe, a polar bear. In the next century, due to conversations about the ethics of enclosed space, most of the large animals were transported to larger zoos, or died. There are now mostly small animals in the Jardin des Plantes' outside enclosures, such as ostriches and flamingos, some grazing creatures, small red pandas cavorting in the Napoleonic bear pit. But still, there are the glasshouses with a metallic framework, such as the Rotonde des Singes, constructed in 1934 in the art deco style, like a glass palace for primates, where two sides can view each other: man watching ape, ape watching man. Much as John Berger writes in a 1991 essay on visiting the zoo in Basel, Switzerland, this open design makes the architecture of the monkey house feel like theater-in-the-round, with multitiered seating (as well as balconies from which the actors can urinate), and makes more pronounced the sensation that the great apes are pantomiming for an audience. It is a strange theater, he writes, where on either side of the glass, each group might think it is the audience. The word *evolution*, Berger goes on, is from the Latin for *unfolding*, and his essay on watching the monkeys at the zoo folds and unfolds in strange and surprising ways, traveling back in history to become a meditation on time. He remembers going to the zoo as a child, with his parents, especially his father. In fact, he tells us that this is one of his spare happy memories of childhood, but doesn't tell us if that's because his memories of childhood are not happy or, just as likely, too many decades have passed for him to remember. There is perhaps no more pronounced a gap of awareness and experience between child and adult than when visiting the zoo. As Berger has written elsewhere, what a child experiences as curious or joyful when looking at the animals—and Berger has his doubts that this is the case—the philosophical adult observes with melancholy, and often a burst of empathy for the oppressed dailiness of the creatures behind bars, a feeling that dissipates somewhat when they're out of sight, for zoos are incredibly complex psychic spaces that are more often than not deeply sad, an odd choice for regular pilgrimages of fun. And yet, Berger remembers sitting as a child with his father, watching the monkeys at play, and pondering a sense of mystery, as he writes, around the unfolding of evolution, especially—as is the cliché—the links between ourselves and the apes, the drama of a 99 percent resemblance. He and his father would lose all sense of time, Berger writes, sitting there in a comfortable silence. He repeats this phrase, lost to the passage of time, blinking back to his present day, an old man in a foreign country amid animated youngsters and their families, traveling back to his London childhood, to when his parents were alive. As Gillian Osborne has noted, one paragraph at the end of the essay startles in its pathos of the critic remembering his stuffed chimpanzee that he received when he was two years old. This paragraph comes suddenly in the midst of a recitation of facts about the evolution of animal locomotion, the accidents that become natural selection, like the aleatory movement of this essay, how the anatomy of apes evolved to allow them to hang from trees and swing from branch to branch, a type of movement known as brachiation, which he depicts in writing in a series of sequences that resemble Eadweard Muybridge's sole-yet-somehow-multiple baboon walking on all fours and climbing up a pole. He remembers as a very small child greeting every visitor to his family's London home with his stuffed chimp, named Jackie, and this is the pathetic gesture in this paragraph, this sequence of memories, toddler John Berger moving across time; just like the toddlers he's observing at the zoo in Basel, he moves into the darkroom of his memory and cannot say for sure that the stuffed monkey was named Jackie. The only one who would really know for sure is his mother, and his mother is dead. Perhaps there is the smallest chance—the same one-in-a-million chance, he notes, as a genetic mutation by natural selection—that a reader will be able to tell him that they were one of the many visitors to his home back in his youth, who went through his door, to this room of his childhood. It is this attempt to beseech or connect to the reader that is one of the many moving and strange moments in this passage, not only the mother who flits a spectral presence throughout, more in periphery than the father, but the slippages of memory: Can anyone remember me? Can I even remember myself? Both faces are pressed up to the glass in this moment—the author's and the reader's—and it's unclear who is the performer and who is the audience. The true meditation comes to the surface here: that of an awareness of mortality, and wondering whether monkeys share that same existential dread. The toddler clutching his stuffed monkey, now an old man, finds himself looking at his reflection in a mirror, that of an older gorilla who appears to be almost blind, which he compares to Samuel Beckett's Pozzo, who chooses not to see, as opposed to having to think about time, or the inevitability of his death. He asks the young zookeeper what the age is of the elder gorilla, and she regards him, as if with pity, and tells him that they're about the same age, a moment that does seem like it is out of a Beckett play. What do people think of this man in his early sixties alone—if he is in fact alone—at the zoo on an autumn day? And regarding a sepia-toned photograph of the Rotonde des Singes at the Jardin des Plantes—I note the one stark tree in the center of the enclosure that seems to be the stage design for a simian production of *Waiting for Godot*, theatergoers in their Sunday finest waiting around for something to happen, with the performers inside, uncertain of their roles. Vladimir Nabokov reportedly first felt the flash of inspiration for *Lolita* after reading a newspaper account of an ape in the Jardin des Plantes, one that apparently produced the first drawing by an animal, a charcoal sketch of the bars of its cage, one of many historical accounts of orangutans on exhibition trained to imitate human skills, much like Berger's reference to the chimps in the London Zoo he saw as a child in the 1930s, who pantomimed eating and drinking. In the 1600s, Dutch physician Jacobus Bontius wrote of wild apes on the island of Java called *Ourang Outang*, or *man of the forest*. There were also secondhand accounts of early European explorers encountering wild human-like creatures in the forest, finding them both familiar and unfamiliar at the same time, living thousands of miles away, inside African and Asian jungles, with even those such as Rousseau wondering if they were a separate, mysterious race of wild men.

For two and a half centuries, a number of orangutans were dissected, when dead, in anatomical laboratories, and a few of the juveniles, taken from their mothers, were kept alive in zoos, where a majority of them died after only a couple of years from human illnesses—or perhaps something else, such as in the case of three-year-old Jenny, dressed in proper girls' clothes and kept in the heated giraffe enclosure at the London Zoo, and whose cage a twenty-nine-year-old Charles Darwin climbed into in an attempt to observe her emotional life, finding her throwing a tantrum like a naughty child when refused an apple, only to eat the fruit contentedly in her chair once she got what she wanted. He ran experiments on Jenny and another young ape named Tommy, giving them mirrors, which fascinated them, and tickling them, observing them capable of jealousy, sulking, and play, recording notes in what are known as his "transmutation notebooks." Young Jenny died after less than two years in captivity, of an unspecified illness, although the conditions of her captivity, including the inability to move freely or exist in her preferred climate, and feelings of estrangement from her natural habitat, along with her isolation from other apes, were likely contributing factors. It is difficult not to look upon the fate of young Jenny with what we know now of an orangutan's capacity for self-recognition and awareness of the continuity of the self over time, as shown by the cognitive experiments performed on Bornean orangutans in Tokyo, who were documented as being able to discriminate between previously and recently recorded videos of themselves. "Every animal searches, only apes research," writes Berger. This curiosity makes them suffer, he observes—from an overwhelming lassitude that he characterizes as ennui, after Baudelaire, when deprived of events or spectators. This is only the state, one can imagine, of captive apes who have learned to cathect onto the humans that keep them—or perhaps this boredom is our own projection, and is somehow linked as a term to how humans keep animals, including in the cage of our own language. Boredom, or the appearance of inertia, makes zookeepers nervous, as it deprives the ticket buyers of spectacle. Perhaps this is why so much is made of the arrival of a new baby, an event that interrupts the dailiness of the monkey house. Berger, swinging from branch to branch, moves to the maternal spectacle, the matrilineal reproductive labor of the monkeys, which gives them relief from their tedium, when the younger females cradle the babies, the ongoing and pleasurable, even aggressive, ritual of grooming that he remembers his mother observing, possibly finding her own moment of recognition. Even the act of brachiation has evolved so the young can fall into the arms of their mothers with a yelp, a moment in the essay that punctures with its own poignant cry, of memory, of mommy. He observes the mother orangutan cradling her baby like out of a Cosimo Tura Madonna and Child, a tenderness, dare he say, that he defensively adds, in a fragmented, elliptical moment, isn't an indulgence in sentimental confusion.

I am reminded of my visit to the menagerie at the Jardin des Plantes several years ago, when I found myself standing outside of the monkey house with my then two-year-old daughter, who was in a travel stroller. Approaching the monkey house always feels chaotic, with the sounds of monkeys as they swing in a complex geometry of ropes and pulleys and trees, or tree-like structures, in the outside enclosures that are still enclosed, so are at once outside-inside. I became aware of an older woman who had been following us, whom I assumed worked at the zoo, so knowledgeable was she of the well-being of all of the monkeys, although she wasn't wearing a zoo uniform. She told us, in English, to go inside and see a wonderful surprise. Inside the ancient dark singerie we saw the flashes of light and heard the clicking of camera shutters as people took pictures of a massive orangutan lying on a bed of straw and fabric, cradling a very tiny baby who had just been born that week, whose name I later learned was Java. So this was all of the excitement, I remember thinking, also that I wished she had privacy, even though I too was staring and desiring to glimpse this special sight with my daughter. How tired she is, I remember thinking, looking at the mother, whose name was Theodora. Milky, I said to my daughter, using the sign for milk, the clasping and unclasping of the hand, and she understood. The baby was latched on. As I write this, the baby, my second daughter, is on me like a monkey, and I am the weary, mammoth one, covered in folds of skin, whom she reaches up to nurse on. In the singerie, my now older daughter and I watched for a while, the stasis of the mother and child, its silent vibrations, but the darkness, offset by flashes of light and sounds, became too much for me, and we walked outside, where I found myself, still disoriented, stepping over a large tranquilizer gun brought by one of the zoo vets, who was approaching an extremely large orangutan with sagging breasts and a burnished orange mane, who I realized later was the famous Nénette, the matriarch of a troop of five orangutans rescued from poachers in the forest of Borneo and arriving at the zoo in 1972, spending nearly her entire life in captivity. She trusts him, the woman said to me, as she was suddenly behind us again now, also watching the daily administrations of Nénette, as if this was a regular ritual for her. Since then, I have watched a documentary of Nénette in which the camera steadies on everyone clustered at the glass, murmuring often quite rude and sometimes philosophical meditations at the taciturn ape. It is something about her expressive face that makes her resemble a silent film tragedienne, somehow. Bontius reported that the Javanese claimed that these humanimal-like creatures could talk but stayed silent because they were afraid of being enslaved into work. She is an old lady, the woman at the monkey house said of Nénette, as the orangutan had just turned fifty, living much longer than she was expected to in captivity. When she told me this, I wondered how old this woman was, perhaps not much older than the ape, like a mirroring moment out of Berger's essay on ape theater. And even now, as I'm gathering up these notes, I experience the slipperiness of time, as this was several years ago, even though I've meant to record these memories for some time, and I realize I am closer in age to the Nénette I saw then, who I thought was so ancient.

Since then, I've witnessed other encounters of older women devotedly visiting the primate enclosures at zoos. In August 2021, a Belgian woman by the name of Adie Timmermans was effectively banned from making any more contact with a thirty-eight-year-old male chimp named Chita, after visiting him at the Antwerp Zoo every week for four years, saying goodbye by pressing her face against the glass for Chita to come in for a kiss. Chita was previously kept as a pet until, thirty years ago, he arrived at the zoo after being abandoned because his behavior was deemed unmanageable. Because of this, he was more accustomed to human companionship than the other chimps, calling to mind one of the cautionary tales of the 1970s chimp-language experiments, that of Nim Chimpsky, part of a Columbia University research study. Raised in a family and taught sign language, Nim was carried around on his surrogate mother's hip for two years, until he began breaking things around the Manhattan brownstone and biting once he entered his terrible twos, only eventually to be abandoned to live an institutionalized life in cages with other chimps sold to a medical laboratory. Perhaps this was also the tragedy of Chita, raised with blankets and soft toys, in diapers and with bottles, and then forced to live as a chimp on hard surfaces the rest of his life. Herbert Terrace, the lead psychologist for Project Nim, deemed Nim Chimpsky incapable of making language to form his own sentences and ideas, using his namesake's definition of communication, instead insisting that he could only use signs as a form of mimicry. J. M. Coetzee's alter ego, Elizabeth Costello, lectures on Kafka's Red Peter, an ape who has learned to mimic the language and mannerisms of his captors as a form of survival, seeing this fictional character as the first of the great apes to really speak. Costello hypothesizes that the inspiration for Red Peter was the chimp Sultan, one of the brightest subjects of psychologist Wolfgang Köhler's experiments at the Anthropoid Station on the island of Tenerife in the early 1900s, which were devoted to understanding the mental capacities of chimpanzees. Sultan was particularly adept at solving problems to try to get the bananas just out of his reach, including by climbing up on stacked crates. In her lecture, Costello attempts to trace his thoughts. "The question that truly occupies him, as it occupies the rat and the cat and every other animal trapped in the hell of the laboratory or the zoo, is: 'Where is home, and how do I get there?'" Perhaps this is why Kafka's Red Peter chooses the life of the music hall over the zoo, even though, despite the convivial atmosphere, he remains isolated, neither human nor totally animal, going home at night to mate with a poor chimpanzee chosen for him who does not speak.

A primatologist was interviewed in *The New York Times* about Francis Bacon's 1957 painting *Study for Chimpanzee*, which, the scientist notes, looks more like a baboon than a chimpanzee, or at least like a blurry figure somewhere between human and primate, and was more likely than not inspired by one of Muybridge's baboons, as Bacon painted from photographs that littered the floor of his chaotic studio, or perhaps was gleaned from *Introducing Monkeys*, a strange photobook by V. J. Stanek, the director of the Prague Zoo. She noted that there was something so unhappy about the sight of a chimp sitting by himself, as chimps are incredibly social creatures. This is why zookeepers have separated Adie Timmermans from Chita. A spokesperson for the zoo said they wanted to make sure he could be a chimpanzee among chimpanzees, since a primate that associates too much with humans is often isolated from the group, or his peers, as they put it. Chita already had trouble integrating into the chimpanzee troupe and was injured as part of a 2008 brawl. As a result of Chita's kissy-face with Timmermans (and perhaps others), he spent all day sitting alone outside of zoo hours, shunned by his fellow apes, waiting for visitors, which does in its way conjure Francis Bacon's study, which is likely a study of a photograph, although Bacon did visit the monkey enclosures at the London Zoo, perhaps with his friend Isabel Rawsthorne. Bacon's triptych of Rawsthorne portraits has a simian quality, and she herself drew the baboons while visiting the zoo. Something about the redhead in the Bacon Rawsthorne looks like Adie Timmermans, suffering, heartbroken. "I haven't got anything else," Timmermans said to reporters. "Why do they want to take that away?" Bacon's paintings are supposed to symbolize the agony of man, his primal scream, underneath the suited surface appearance. When describing his animal studies, Bacon has said that "we nearly always live through screens—a screened existence," as if prescient of a current time when chimps from two separate Czech zoos look at giant Zoom screens of each other throughout the day, to keep company during a duration when they cannot interact with human visitors, videos which then live stream on the zoo's website in order to bring in visitors, if only virtually. It would appear that captive primates have inherited our boredom, what Mark Fisher, in his work on capitalist realism, calls our collective "depressive hedonia," or the modern affliction of needing constant stimulation through screens. They seemed so bored, my students say, of the large apes in their enclosures, and I teasingly ask them if they are aware of the intensity of their lassitude, in their boxes or cages, over Zoom while listening to me lecture on bored monkeys, their sometimes-frozen faces from bad connections resembling a Francis Bacon portrait.

I connect the episode at the monkey house in Paris to one that took place sometime later, at the baboon enclosure at the Prospect Park Zoo, where once again I found myself conversing with an older woman who seemed intimately aware of the daily life of these great apes. Or should I say that once again I found a woman conversing with me, following me, as I scooted along the glass with the stroller, which I had managed to get down the stairs, watching the hierarchies of the harem of hamadryas baboons and watching the young ones play and fight, taking rides on their mothers' backs, grooming each other. As before, I found myself being polite while wondering why she was speaking to me, and why she seemed to know so much about the baboons. Was she a docent or a volunteer? As before, it left me with an odd and lingering feeling. She told me and my daughter, who could speak a little and ask questions, that when the weather is bad, baboons often watch television in indoor facilities. I don't know why she would know this if she didn't work there. Ever since, I always imagine that all of the animals that can't be seen are watching television—often, as I've read, videos of other monkeys, like the bonobos at a German zoo who could choose three options of viewing pleasure: watching primates eat, play, or mate; surprisingly for the hypersexual bonobos, the last was not the most popular option. The baboon enclosure at the Prospect Park Zoo has tiered seating, much like Berger documents in Basel, and when my daughter was very young, as young as when Berger first had Jackie, we would regularly visit the dimly lit monkey house. My daughter would often press up against the glass, along with the other children, trying to see the monkeys scurry across from a suspended height. I always marveled at the markings of the male hamadryas baboons, whose remarkable silver manes resemble to me the stiff collar in an old master painting, like Velázquez's *Philip IV*, and there's an aptness to this reference, since the monarch presided over most of the Thirty Years' War, and baboons are prone to violent and destructive wars, even more extreme than the chimpanzee war that Jane Goodall observed in Gombe, or recalling Chita beaten up by his fellow chimpanzees in Antwerp. I believe one of the last times we went to see the baboons, if not the very last time, was when we witnessed an extremely bloody fight breaking out between two older males, which became so scary for the children watching that we went and sought out someone who worked at the zoo in order to tell them, and were informed that a new troupe of baboons had been placed within the enclosure and that the fight was over territory. It was only later, while conducting research on what the conditions of the London Zoo might have been like when Berger visited as a child, that I learned of the massive and ongoing conflict in the early 1930s at the London Zoo's Monkey Hill, an outdoor enclosure like a large rock that mimicked not only their native habitat but also the outdoor exhibits of the Hagenbeck Zoo, which promised fresh air and space for their primates—as opposed keeping them inside in the dark, sickly and bored—while also providing a better show. Kafka's Red Peter, captured by a Hagenbeck safari, chose the music hall to avoid ending up at Hagenbeck, and in *Minima Moralia,* Adorno, in a passage on the zoological garden as not only a site of imprisonment but also nineteenth-century colonial imperialism, takes on the apparently humane open layout of Hagenbeck, with trenches and no bars: "The more invisible the boundaries become," he writes, "the more completely the freedom of the creatures is repudiated, whose gaze could be ignited by the longing for the wide distance." In 1925, a shipment of approximately one hundred baboons arrived at the London Zoo by boat from the Horn of Africa—most of them male, but six female; the males were preferred because of their dramatic and gaudy coloring, without anyone from the Hagenbeck cluing the Zoological Society of London in to their extremely patriarchal society. Because they were kept in a relatively small enclosure, this resulted in a bloodbath, and over their first few years at the zoo, when Berger would have been a small child, their numbers dwindled to just a few. Perhaps this is why Berger's mother didn't like to go with them to see the monkeys. "I sometimes think, when people say my work looks violent, that perhaps I have from time to time been able to clear away one or two of the veils or screens," said Francis Bacon. When was the last time we've been to the monkey house? It must have been before everything closed down. We've been to that zoo since then, but have remained outside, avoiding the inside. It feels like so long since we've been inside anywhere at all. Did we stop going to them because of the startling violence we witnessed there, or simply because the animals were too sad? Have the monkeys been okay since we've been away?

THE WINTER ZOO

We returned to the zoo during the winter break. The city, or at least our surrounding neighborhoods, appeared emptied out, possibly to extended family or island holidays. My sister had gifted us a membership, and so our entry was free. We had nothing else to do after the toddler woke up from her nap and before the early winter darkness fell. Maybe we were curious to see how the animals were faring, this season, during the changing temperatures. We entered the zoo from the Children's Corner, which led us directly to the sea lion pool. Each time we visited that winter, we just missed the last feeding of the day, where zoo workers, usually women, feed their charges from buckets of fish, encouraging them to turn flips or clap large sleek flippers to their human hands, to the applause of the crowd. The zoo's website for the sea lion feeding hours had not been updated since March 2020, as if our ensuing isolation had frozen the schedule, and by the time we arrived, we were told feeding was just over for the day. Still, we would stick around, peering over the rails that so many children try to climb on top of, and probably have since the zoo was built almost a century ago, watching the creatures swim around and around, in that sleek, undulating way, the typical pattern for pinnipeds in captivity, though they can travel thousands of miles in the wild. On one visit, the only other child who was there found a small inert fish on the pavement and, after a zoo worker gave permission, tossed it into the pool. One of the sea lions swiftly retrieved it and gobbled it up, then swam over close to us, almost to the railing, as though it were peering at us with inquisitive eyes set apart in a whiskered face. My youngest, at their eye level in the stroller, kept referring to them as dogs. Although at two, she knows the word *sea lion*, having played with a plastic sea lion figurine in the bath, the same figurine she placed in a state of unusual solitude on my desk while I was working on this report, perhaps having heard me ask her father how he would describe the architectural layout of the zoo. Maybe she cannot match the plastic replica with the immensity of the actual animal.

The sea lions seemed eager to see us. It is possible they felt something was off, because of the disappearing winter crowds, and decreased public feedings, or because of the encroaching darkness during that time of day. These events—the multiple daily feedings, the attention—structured their time, as well as providing stimulation, and the sea lions most likely intuited a loss, when time changed and there was darkness and the human beings disappeared so early, a change that was winter but couldn't be experienced according to the natural rhythms of such. I read that sea lions often eat more when it gets colder, fortifying themselves with an increased fat intake and the resulting layers of blubber. Perhaps seeing tiny humans gather around them again made them wonder if more food was coming.

I have become fascinated with the ways in which this zoo, like so many others, has been remodeled over the century into what is now known as a children's zoo. The open-air sea lion pool has remained the focal point of the zoo's central semicircular, fan-like layout. Online I find an undated, tinted photographic postcard of that same pool, which originally held seals, surrounded by a crowd. Judging by the fact that all the men are wearing hats, it must have been taken before the 1960s. Robert Moses used the Works Progress Administration funds to build this new zoo in 1935, which then held a bear pit, a lion house, a monkey house, and soon afterwards, elephants, housed in the dome-shaped Animal Lifestyles building. Like the other brick and limestone animal buildings in the zoo, all of them designed by the architect Aymar Embury II, it bears a stone relief from Rudyard Kipling's *The Jungle Book*. It now houses, among a variety of tropical and nocturnal birds, monkeys ranging from tiny frowning tamarins to larger and more aggressive baboons. In another online photograph, from a personal archive of childhood photos from the 1960s, a lone baby elephant is hanging around outside the building, on an elevated step, almost as if out in the open air, except for what appears to be two horizontal wires, although it's possible, as it's been recently pointed out to me, these are just creases in the photograph, and I'm imagining these signs of the elephant's captive state. Still there is a barrenness and heartbreaking sense of isolation to this amateur photograph of the brown elephant alone amidst brick and concrete.

It's difficult to tell what season it is in the tinted postcard. Everyone is wearing a coat, but the forest behind them, and the grass in the foreground, are lush and green. Perhaps it is that cold period of early spring, or a cold snap in fall before the leaves change. The density of the crowd blocks our view of the pinnipeds that the people are intently watching. They must be just swimming down in the pool, as they do, diving to the only depths they can find in that shallow pool. Within the *animal display industry*, I read online, sea lions and seals are popular for exhibits, especially seal shows. Among the *pinnipeds in captivity*, sea lions are becoming even more popular to exhibit than seals. The seals perhaps have more tricks, but the sea lions, on the whole, are more gregarious, in groups of their own and with people.

When we came to the zoo in summer, it was so crowded around the pool that it was difficult to see, and I had to hoist the oldest up. There was an announcer then, near the entrance, with a microphone and a speaker. I wondered whether this was stressful for the sea lions; I had once read, I don't remember where, that the animals were often stressed by the din of the congested traffic sounds on Flatbush Avenue. I wondered what sea lions, and the other animals, made of the scarcity of visitors during the winter. It must not have been too different from how it was when the zoo had been closed to the public during lockdown. On our winter visits, the zoo workers seemed to be more relaxed than in the summer, freer to be themselves. I found myself observing them, wondering what it was like to take care of the animals, to feed them, in the quiet winter zoo. My children were often noisier than the animals.

The second time we were at the sea lion court during winter break was a late afternoon in January. It had warmed up, and we were unsure how many layers of clothing we needed. It was a bright day, and the three sea lions were on the rocks, clumped together, an unusual sighting when there wasn't a show. One of them was resting her chin on the sleek body of another. They were most likely gathered together for warmth. I am calling the sea lion *her* because of something I was told by a child who was visiting the zoo that day with her mother. The child, who attended the same school as my kindergartener, and was a few grades older, was eager to share her knowledge about the sea lions. She told us the ones at this zoo are females, and the ones at the Bronx Zoo are males. I imagined, when she was telling me this, that a separation happened at one point, because of territorial behavior that was less than optimal for the exhibit crowds. The girl also told us the names of the sea lions we were watching, which I've now forgotten. (Later I looked up her claim; actually, male and female sea lions are not separated at these two zoos.) We all watched the sea lions vocalizing loudly on the rocks. They're making so much noise, I remarked to this child. Why were they being so loud? She didn't know either, and seemed, like me, somewhat disturbed. We stood there for a while staring at the three sea lions, who were staring back at us. Afterward, I read about the communication styles of the sea lion, their barking and honking. The sea lions appeared to be roaring at us, but not, it seemed, in an unfriendly way. Although I've also read the roar is usually a request to be left alone.

While standing there I looked over at the bronze sculpture at the base of the twin staircase, near the Flatbush Avenue entrance, *Lioness and Cubs*, created in 1899 by the French animalier Victor Peter. I always look for it whenever we are at the sea lions exhibit. However—this is most likely a trick of my mind—I swear that when my eldest was a toddler, it was in a different location around the pool. I'm not sure exactly where. I have a memory of my daughter at four playing there with her friend of the same age, during a late winter, climbing the sculpture and sliding down, with hardened filthy snow that hadn't yet melted surrounding it. Apparently, I read later,

Robert Moses had moved the statue inside the zoo from the park to prevent children from doing just that. This must have been one of the first trips to the zoo the first winter after everything shut down, when we stayed outside of the main buildings, a habit that persisted, I'm not sure why. It wasn't only because of fear of contagion, but most likely because it felt depressing and claustrophobic, being inside the zoo buildings, watching the animals from behind glass, and it felt better, somehow, to be out in the open air. It was easier for me to look at the statue of the tiny cubs nursing on their mother, and think about how time and space had collapsed, than to pay attention to the honking creatures in front of us.

I visited the zoo regularly when my now six-year-old was between two and three, around the age my youngest is now, and it feels almost uncanny to keep returning to the same place. Maybe, like most people at the zoo, my gaze takes in the animals and their captivity, and then turns toward the other spectators. I see myself among the others, looking back at them, which makes it impossible for me to truly relax. While thinking through this I look through various digitized photographs of the zoo online at the Brooklyn

Public Library. There is one photo from the 1950s of children watching a lioness in a cage, in the same pose as the serene lioness in Victor Peter's statue. The zoo's literature likes to historicize the evolution of styles and attitudes of confinement over the century, to show the progress. In 1890 an informal menagerie opened in the park's Long Meadow. It had a bear pit, complete with three bears. An entry from the 1896 annual report lists the livestock owned by the parks department: fifty-nine sheep, twenty-eight deer, one buffalo, one cow, three bears, one puma, two raccoons, ten rabbits, one dog, one eagle, eight pea fowls, eight doves, thirty-nine Chinese geese, fifteen Egyptian geese, seven Muscovy ducks, four common ducks, and three turkeys, often housed in cramped cages, or grazing behind wire fences. A colorized photograph shows Victorian-era buggies and woman in bustle dresses and men in formal wear peering into wooden cages. We can't see the animals, as the focus is on the humans. More animals were eventually acquired from other zoos and private collections, including zebras, elephants, and baboons. In 1900, the zoo both opened an aviary and, according to the July 8 *Brooklyn Daily Eagle*, added one Columbian black-tailed deer, one pronghorn antelope, five swift foxes, two gray wolves, six woodchucks, two red foxes, four American flamingos, one dusky horned owl, and two coral snakes. The menagerie transformed into a zoo with the purchase of seventy animals from the remaining collection of the circus mogul Frank Bostock, who had a live animal show at Dreamland, the old amusement park at Coney Island, until it was decimated by a fire in 1911. Soon after, Bostock died of a stroke. The *Brooklyn Daily Eagle* spearheaded a donation campaign that allowed anyone who purchased an animal to rename it. The paper published a daily list urging Brooklyn residents to contribute toward the two thousand dollars that needed to be raised before November 11, 1914, the day the animals were to arrive in Prospect Park.

More naturalistic habitats without the obvious appearance of bars began to replace cages and pits, modeled after the Hagenbeck Zoo in Hamburg, Germany. One might argue that these less restrictive environments were put in place more to appease the public and less to eliminate the inhumane conditions. The animals were still captive and not able to roam freely. A few decades ago, the polar bears would have been kept in an enclosure where an administration building now stands, behind the sea lion pool. There they hung out on the rocks that resemble large boulders or icebergs. One evening in 1987, three boys broke into the zoo after hours, planning to swim in the moat in the polar bear enclosure. One of the boys, eleven years old, was mauled to death by the two polar bears, thirty-three-year-old Teddy and thirty-two-year-old Lucy, weighing fourteen hundred and nine hundred pounds respectively, who had been sleeping in their faux caves when the presence of the boys woke them up. When the police arrived, they shot and killed the bears. This gruesome incident prompted the phasing out of the large animals in the zoo, leaving only the gregarious sea lions and the territorial baboons, who

are kept behind glass inside the Animal Lifestyles building.

It's important, I feel, to at least partially disassociate when at the zoo, and to avoid thinking of the lives of animals who have lived their entire existences in captivity. One sees the animals through the curious faces of one's children. We lingered like that, in front of the sea lion pool, with our friends, and decided to walk together as a group, along the path, as it grew darker out, the older children running ahead, the toddler toddling after them. That afternoon, as on our previous visit, the peacocks, usually the only animals running about freely, albeit with their legs tagged, were nowhere to be seen. I imagined the cold must have driven the birds inside, to heated shelters. I watched a brilliantly colored bird, a quail or pheasant in a glassed-in enclosure, run around in circles in a corner, as if stuck there. I stared as it repeated this tiny circuit, around and around, around and around, a pacing within captivity known as stereotypic behavior. We stopped to look at the Pallas's cat, who is prowling around and around. The Pallas's cat, used to snowy mountain terrains, is happy, the placard tells us, in freezing temperatures. Or at least their ancestors were, since the animals have been in zoos in the United States for decades, as part of captive breeding programs. The Pallas's cat looks like a big furry house cat. The children are disappointed that the other animals that are happy in the winter, the little red panda, the pair of sea otters, which were there during the previous visit, have already gone inside in preparation for the zoo's closure. Right after Christmas we watched the sea otters chase each other underneath the ice, but then stand on their legs, near the gate to their indoor habitat, as if hoping to be fed or let in for the night. On that first winter zoo visit, on the way to the barn to feed the sheep and llamas, we stopped to watch the blue heron that often flits in the garden near the farm animals. The heron's curious figure delicately rested standing nearly motionless on top of the iced-over pond. When the ice had completely melted, we spotted it again only now it was soaring high up overhead, free to fly away or linger as it pleased.

REPORT FROM THE CITY ZOOS

THE BRONX ZOO

They were inside like we were, during the first atmospheric disturbances of June. The city zoos closed during the orange smog, to minimize, they said, stress to the animals. We had been cooped up as well, sleeping on the floor in a guest room with our two small children, contained living in a temporary residence. I had been hoping to continue my zoo investigations, hoping, somehow, that going there might dispel my bad mood, although I don't know why I thought that. We needed to get outside. Perhaps one goes to the zoo as a way to get fresh air. Although certainly that wasn't the case this time. In a public space the animals existed alongside of us and the smoke, in the atmosphere.

The children had been asking to go, now that school was over. I hadn't been to the zoo since the winter, although they had gone to the Bronx several times with their father, while I taught writing classes all day at a college nearby, sitting at the same chair for six hours at a time. I would receive photographs and videos on my phone, of the children gleeful on the bug carousel, of the giraffes crowded in their house delicately eating leaves from on high. I too felt the quality of being stuffed inside, all winter.

We finally drove to the Bronx, on a Sunday, in Unhealthy Conditions for Sensitive People. I wanted to think about *The Animals*, the photobook by Garry Winogrand, a series of forty-three wide angle black-and-white photographs taken at the various city zoos and the aquarium over a period of seven years, from 1962 to 1969. The plastic-wrapped book had been sent to me at my request by the Fraenkel Gallery in San Francisco at the address I had just moved out of, after living there a decade. Since the book was out of print, I had to promise to return it. The cardboard box in which it was shipped and the book were two of the only objects I took with me, to our temporary residence, until we could move into our new apartment.

We wait for parking in Asia, stopping to have the toddler go pee in a travel potty outside of our ancient compact car, trying to find a place to dump the plastic bag of urine, parking our filthy stroller at the stroller parking. Following the lines, we find ourselves riding the Wild Asia monorail, as it's something the children have never done, usually entering the zoo from the other side. We listen to voice-overs about the near extinction of the Sumatran rhino, the children eager to see the tufted deer, the tiger from on high, glimpsing the solitary, sadly named Happy the Elephant, denied a habeas corpus petition by the New York Supreme Court, to be able to leave the zoo, where she has lived for fifty years, for a sanctuary with other elephants, despite being the first elephant to pass the mirror self-recognition test, despite elephants being social and intelligent animals who need other elephant companions. (Free Happy! a middle-aged person—me—obnoxiously shouts out.) I am reminded of all the elephants in *The Animals*.

There are photographs of elephants humping, juxtaposed across from a human couple on a date. Two elephants waving their trunks at the flank of a rhino, showing their close proximity in captivity. Three photographs, including one that adorns the cover, of a solitary elephant reaching for a hand holding peanuts. An elephant by itself, in front of an enclosure, visited only by a bird. Many of the photographs show the larger animals behind bars, but without the melancholy musical accompaniment of a documentary work like Chris Marker's three-minute slow montage *Zoo Piece*, made in 1994 for French TV, where it's clear the sadness and heavy zoo feelings the artist wants to evoke, the animal in solitary confinement. It's not apparent in Winogrand's project whether he finds zoos sad, like Chris Marker does—the affect is one projected often by the one viewing the photographs, depending on their own zoo feelings.

Much like Winogrand's other series, his zoo project is one of the city; as he has noted, zoos often are in cities. Winogrand grew up in the Pelham Parkway neighborhood within walking distance of the Bronx Zoo. My mother also grew up in the Bronx, in a tenement to the south of the zoo, in a working-class

Jewish family like Winogrand, her father a public hack driver. She died at fifty-six, the same age as Winogrand, although twenty years later, both of a fast cancer. My mother never spoke about her childhood, trying, I believe, to find some distance from its poverty. I often wondered if as a kid she went to that zoo, only a few blocks away. She probably did. What else was there to do?

In his essay on looking at animals, John Berger writes that the family visit to a zoo is banal in its sentimentality, reproducing childhood. I went as a child—I will take my children there. "Adults take children to the zoo to show them the originals of their 'reproductions,' and also in the hope of re-finding some of the innocence of that reproduced animal world that they remember from their own childhood." The zoo gaze is upon your child, watching your children seeing the animals, remembering yourself as a child.

When Garry Winogrand's two children were young, he would take them to the zoo. Mostly, Winogrand has said, he took snapshots with his Leica of his children on these outings, when he had the kids on the weekend, once he was separated from their mother.

Then once he saw something interesting in the contact sheets he began to play with composition, with juxtaposition and tilting the horizon. These are presumably the two children who are doing flips on the railing of the rhino enclosure in one photograph, acting like monkeys, as mine do as well. So much of the experience of flipping through *The Animals* is the juxtaposition of the solitary with the paired, and the human with the animal. The previous diptych, before the two children hanging upside down in front of two butting rhinos, is of gorillas cavorting with each other in their play enclosure, in groups and pairs, hugging, snacking. In two separate photographs, a pair of chimps wave and play on a ladder. This is the sly joke hanging over the play of images across the opening—the children are also the animals. But there's no doubt a banality to these images as well—many are remarkable in their ordinariness.

Disembarking, we collect our stroller and attempt to walk on foot, for as far as we are able, to visit the giraffes grazing outside in the African plains, the day-glo flamingos, outside of the historic beaux arts pavilions, stopping for the promised ice creams, the carousel, the bathroom visits and breakdowns, refusing the stuffed animal swag. We miss the gorillas, the world of birds in the brutalist building, that the children have all seen before. It's impossible to see it all in a day.

Walking with children is the opposite of urban strolling. You are pushing, pulling, shoving, carrying, *trudging*. There's no flânerie at a zoo. Janet Malcolm uses the word "clomping" to imagine Winogrand at work (she was not, by any means, a fan): "Winogrand goes clomping right up to people, as one gathers from the startled or disgusted expressions on the faces of many of his subjects." It's true, people do clump and clomp at the zoo. The real horror, for Malcolm, seems to be Winogrand's lack of elegance and refinement, although it's hard to separate that from the milieus he documented and came from, their working-class sphere. It's all so ugly, so vulgar, so *grotesque*, a word often used in discussion of *The Animals*, including in John Szarkowski's afterword to the now out-of-print book, published by the Museum of Modern Art in conjunction with the inaugural exhibition of the photographs. The judgment of the word, its carnivalesque connotation, might say as much about what these critics think of zoos as what they think of the photographs, for there's nothing particularly grotesque about these photographs, except possibly the emphasis on humping (a leer that matches Winogrand's general divorced dad vibes). For Szarkowski, the zoo used to offer a happy fairy-tale stroll for him and his wife, before he saw in Winogrand's project a lack of recognition and bad feelings, between the human and the animal. The influential MoMA curator of photography first showed a Winogrand zoo photograph in his 1967 *New Documents* show, alongside work by Diane Arbus and Lee Friedlander, the one of the couple talking, their backs to the dog on the other side of the bars, seemingly stalking them, a funny-sad photograph rendered hyperbolically by critics in the language of horror. (Hilton Als writes, "There is, for example, a young couple standing by a cage, seemingly unmindful of the caged beast—their desire?—stalking them on the other side of the bars.")

In her 1975 essay "Certainties and Possibilities," the most the photography critic has written at length about Winogrand, Malcolm compares the series to the horror of Francis Bacon's writhing animals:

[Winogrand] shows the Central Park Zoo for the dirty prison it was, focusing on the bars, the concrete floors, the dispirited, ugly animals, the dumb (for thinking they are enjoying themselves), ugly people, and the grubbiness and meanness, conveying an atmosphere of nakedness and brown-soap harshness like that found in the paintings of Francis Bacon.

The essay is thinking admiringly through Szarkowski's tenure at the MoMA, and about Winogrand as an American arbiter of photography as art, after Robert Frank, laying bare the ugliness and vulgarity of America with his photographs (*ugliness* repeats through Malcolm's essay, in reference to Winogrand—ugliness at "radical angles," maybe initially in an admiring way toward this new realistic aesthetic.) But the tonality of comparing Winogrand's zoo photographs to the psychosexual cruelty of Bacon's frenzied hybrids feels wrong. Or, it really depends upon the viewer and their own projected zoo feelings. Certainly most of the solitary animals don't look happy—there's a melancholy, clownish quality to the close-up of the orangutan eating a spoon of ice cream or yogurt. But I find Winogrand's photographs are more tinged with gentle irony and teasing vulgarity than freighted with a point of view or explicit commentary, for better or for worse. This is partially Malcolm's issue in general with Winogrand's "snapshots," as she's referred to them, their lack of a thesis statement or point of view, or "information," as she calls it in a 2015 conversation with Winogrand enthusiast Geoff Dyer, the interview tracing the arc of her disinterest or disgust. Dyer counters by quoting Szarkowski that a very good Winogrand photograph possesses a "new knowledge."

But what is this new zoo knowledge? Is it, like Szarkowski says, that the animal and human exist in mutual lack of recognition and bad manners? There's a question of whether Winogrand is trying to show the ugliness of the zoo, as Malcolm suggests, or whether there's a tinge of classist horror in looking at him look at zoos, projected toward the enjoyment of the working-class patrons. It's true, there is little glamour to be found in the Bronx Zoo, although the people Winogrand depicted in the 1960s are far more dressed up than the current shorts-wearing horde, whose shabbiness is still in the eye of the critic perceiving them. Working-class families go to this zoo. These are not people who go to rented houses in France or islands in Greece for their summer vacations. Neither were we.

A question that is often asked (including later on, by Peter Schjeldahl) is whether Winogrand's investigations, as he's called them, were pessimistic or optimistic, or whether the photographs simply reflect the times. Did Winogrand like the zoo? asks Szarkowski. This is a good question. Do I like the zoo? Does anyone, above a certain age, actually like the zoo?

Is Winogrand being a "spoilsport" in his realism, Szarkowski asks? In his afterword he depicts the animals in Winogrand's cages of his photographs in little apartments on top of each other, just like us, forced to live in a city, forced into a modern ennui. In reading these photographs, caged animals are often made to represent a modern claustrophobia, as animals are so often made metaphors of the human condition. He doesn't get this from just going to the zoo and looking at the animals, an occasional activity he used to find pleasant—it's the photographs that have now made him see this paralyzed condition in which the animals are forced to live, and he almost wishes not to have this new sight.

Those writing about Winogrand's project often note the boredom or tedium exhibited therein—the animals photographed and then displayed are bored and exhausted, mirroring the crowdgoers' boredom. Within this emphasis is the assumption that the zoo is supposed to be a good time, which is perhaps a carryover from childhood, like memories of the circus, depending on one's age. For most adults, the zoo is extremely tedious. It's more often than not a bad time, like so much child-oriented tourism and entertainment. The zoo in the summer is hot. The animals are uncomfortable. They haven't gotten enough exercise, but neither do they want to walk (I'm talking about the children here).

One begins to wonder how many hours some of these critics have logged lately at the city zoos. Their reactions to the milieu and their overreading of Winogrand's documents of it seem dramatic, heightened, in a way constant exposure tends to make banal. Also, it is often incorrectly stated that the photographs were taken solely at the Central Park Zoo, although they are set also at the Bronx as well as the New York Aquarium in Coney Island.

CENTRAL PARK ZOO

We make it to the Central Park Zoo weeks later on the Fourth of July. It is also the publication date of my new book, which feels so absurd that going to the zoo feels right, as opposed to sitting in a hot apartment refreshing my phone. The weather again tries to resist us—we drive uptown through a flash flood warning, although the rain falling on us, as we walk downstairs into the zoo's entrance in the park, feels like a relief from the steamy heat. I come more prepared this time—I am not a jerk with a camera (Winogrand) but instead a jerk with a little notebook, shoved inside my fanny pack. We join the shorts-wearing hordes, but I note this time, possibly because of the day, or the summer season, possibly because of the milieu, that the fairly sparse zoo attendees seem composed more of tourists wearing expensive, branded clothing (100 percent more Gucci slides than the Bronx Zoo, I note). Because of its location, off of Fifth Avenue and in the leafy park, the small zoo is something you can do in an hour to humor the children, or for a stroll. Like going to the Met. You don't have to really look at a painting or an animal. You don't have to really think whether the gaze looks back at you.

In his essay "The Animals and Their Keepers," Hilton Als reconsiders Winogrand's project in the aftermath of 9/11, as a documentary of New York and of the racial and class and sexual dynamics of the late 1960s. I'm not sure I agree with Hilton Als here that Winogrand is a Dreiser realist, a humanist and not an ironist, or really that Winogrand is telling a specific story or using the zoo as a metaphor. But it undoubtedly feels important to situate Winogrand, as Als does, as a working-class New Yorker, and the zoo as an essential part of the city.

In most of the essay Als performs an involved reading of probably the most famous Winogrand photograph: a movie-star handsome couple, a Hitchcock blonde with a paisley scarf in her hair and a Black man in a tailored gray suit, both carrying chimps dressed like children in hooded sweatshirts, gaze averted as if to resist the paparazzi. (It's unclear whether these are their pets, or whether, as I have wondered, they somehow picked them up from the chimp exhibit. Zoos commonly held "tea parties" for the chimpanzees to entertain audiences, even into the 1960s.) This 1967 photograph, labeled simply Central Park Zoo, is often what is recalled when thinking of Winogrand's zoo project, but it isn't actually, as Als suggests, in the 1969 book *The Animals*. Als, like many critics, reads this and the other zoo photographs as a potent political analogy about the anxieties of miscegenation, about captivity as a metaphor for the racial and even gendered segregation of 1960s New York, focusing also on the image of a Black man holding a cigarette, considering a rhino within spare distance across the barrier, a rare mirrored photograph in the book. For Als, we project onto the photographs our anxieties, revealing underneath the man as beast, both the viewer and the viewed. "In the photograph," Als writes, "we see a white woman and a Black man, apparently a couple, holding the product of their most unholy of unions: monkeys. In projecting what we will into this image—about miscegenation, our horror of difference, the forbidden nature of Black men with white women—we see the beast that lies in us all."

• • •

When Winogrand took the famous photograph in 1967 he was accompanied by his friend Tod Papageorge, who took a similar, less iconic photograph of the same scene, both stimulated, as Papageorge writes later, by its strangeness (this is also Malcolm's issue with Winogrand, as she complains to Dyer of this twinning—who says one photograph of the same scene is any better, or different?) Winogrand didn't actually include it in *The Animals*; despite the overt ridiculousness of the scene, it's possible that its staged-feeling composition departed from the light or accidental quality of the series—the interplay of enclosure, humans, and animals in the space of the zoo, as well as in the space of a photograph. It was just too composed. Papageorge muses, in a later reflection, that while he saw a joke, Winogrand saw a photograph that was laden with meaning and metaphor, which doesn't entirely fit with how Winogrand has spoken about his process, or photography. In *The Animals* there are more gentle and humorous parallels and juxtapositions, gestures that show connections and disconnections; gorillas hugging each other, elephants humping, rhinos sleeping near each other, people talking and ignoring the animals, the uncanny resemblance of a young woman in a leopard coat attempting to make the tongue-in-cheek gesture of the llama in front of her. The mischievous photos tend not to offer easy interpretation, despite a reliance on metaphor when professional lookers have looked at them. "What is the subject of a photograph but a photograph?" Winogrand has been often quoted as saying. Certainly not the animals, although this is possibly the point.

This is John Berger's thesis in "Why Look at Animals?" in his book *About Looking*. Though Berger doesn't deal much with zoo photography in that 1980 essay, which is mainly concerned with our alienation from animals in the history of capitalism, enfolded in the complicated history of zoos, it's a Winogrand that graces the paperback cover (several of the illustrations are black-and-white reproductions of the paintings of Gilles Aillaud, as if to make them look more like zoo photographs, giving a photocopied, archival quality to the entire book that predates W. G. Sebald). The cover of *About Looking* was, Geoff Dyer has said, his first exposure to Winogrand's work, a photograph of people leaning over a curved railing toward a dark blot down below, of a "seal or walrus." It's a walrus! Yet it doesn't seem to matter what animal it is, to Dyer. Berger suggests that animals are actually marginal to the zoo experience, and that marginality seems to me to be the the focus (or lack of focus) of Winogrand's project, whether consciously or not. You don't actually see the animals in the zoo photograph, or at the zoo itself. The experience is a lack of recognition between the animals on either side of the bars. "The zoo to which people go to meet animals, to observe them, to see them, is, in fact, a monument to the impossibility of such encounters," Berger writes. To make a metaphor of the animal is also to ignore the animal (Donna Haraway writes that "we polish an animal mirror when we look for ourselves"). Is the disembodied elephant's trunk stretched out to greet a disembodied open hand for peanuts a sincere moment of connection, or of disconnection? The backs of the animals are to us, or to the backs of humans. The scenes are denatured.

What is more photographed than a zoo? Perhaps a carousel, but they are also animals, if wooden, and frequently zoo-adjacent. And most zoo photographs are bad—out of focus, literal, cliché. Similarly, the effect of *The Animals* (the book) is a series of caged animals and exhibits, some people—like the often boring, sometimes absurd experience of going to a zoo. For Berger, "the view is always wrong. Like an image out of focus." Here he is speaking of zoos, but he could also be speaking of photographs of zoos, including in Winogrand's complicated project that offers no easy thesis, as well as the lack of active zoo thinking in critics looking at Winogrand's series, the lack of reciprocity and recognition looking at the animals. For critics it seems easier to think seriously about photographs than it is to think about the zoo itself. And perhaps, as Berger suggests, the zoo is a place we go, and can only tolerate if we don't really look at it. That tension provides a depth underneath Winogrand's photographs that on their surface seem comic or carnivalesque. The surface lightness belies an existential heaviness.

I try to take photographs of my children smooshed up against the glass of the penguins in their phosphorescent, crowded enclosure with the fake painted-sky backdrop. The competition for iPhone selfies, using the animals as backdrop. (Winogrand makes a teasing commentary on the precursor of this, in his photograph of the old woman wanting her photograph taken in front of the zebra, which becomes pure background.) Most of the time I don't take the photo. Can't spot the snow leopard or red panda against their artificial outside environment (too hot). The snow monkeys are hiding in a cave from the rain. It is because animals are marginalized, Berger writes, that they go toward the edges of their enclosures. Perhaps, toward the edges, the animals can be, if not free, out of sight from the crowds of onlookers. For a moment there is a crowd at the mountainous grizzly bear enclosure. Everyone is gathering around—for what? Are they finally really seeing an animal? One of the two grizzly bears is so hot that he is sprawled out on a rock in front of us. Everyone is chatting and laughing and taking photos. It feels like a Winogrand moment, the bear too sleepy to realize what he's stirred up. Who are we all connecting with? Not the bear. Yet we are all together, in a crowd, us on one side, the bear on the other.

DISAPPEARING ACTS

We begin the essay with an uncited photograph from history. Roland Barthes speaks of photographs of children from history, their innocence and morbidity. To look at an old photograph of children is to look at children who are long dead. But the same is true for archival photographs of zoo animals. What do you see when you look at this photograph? A grouping of children in Victorian dress on top of a very large elephant, with a man keeping the whole contraption at a standstill. From what can possibly be read of the expressions of children from a grainy photograph, they look expectant, excited—the child zoo feeling. The elephant's expression is far more inscrutable. Exhausted, possibly. Or just present. So present that photographs of this famous elephant from history always emphasize how much its extremely mammoth body fills the entire frame, or has been herded into a small enclosure (in fact, anything large began to be called *jumbo* because of the dissemination of his absurdly large likeness in advertisements). Why does John Berger begin with a photograph of Jumbo the Elephant giving rides to children at the London Zoo? Perhaps to situate the Eurocentric nineteenth-century zoo attitude, a narrative of colonialism and alienation from labor (absent while present), a story of tragedy and absurdity, the only possible tonal registers for the history of capitalism. Below is a much clearer photograph than Berger opens with, and the expressions on the faces of the one female chaperone and the children, and the familiar male zookeeper, are far more squinted and uncertain, but it's unclear whether that's due to the extremely large animal they are astride or to the even less familiar performative moment of photography.

Let me tell you a bit more than John Berger does, a story of Jumbo the Elephant, the most famous elephant in history. This is cobbled together from various reports, including David Attenborough's 2017 documentary. The details often conflict. A male African bush elephant, his mother was killed by ivory poachers and big game hunters around the year 1860, somewhere near the Sudan–Eritrea border.

Her tusks were hacked off the carcass to sell. The baby calf was captured and imported first to the Jardin des Plantes in Paris, then transferred to the London Zoo, exchanged for one rhino, one kangaroo, one possum, a jackal, a pair of eagles, and two dingoes. The young elephant had to be nursed back to health upon arrival by his keeper Matthew Scott, pictured, who would sleep in his cage. He had a rotten tail and hoofs, his hide was covered in sores, as Scott writes in his autobiography, "I thought I never saw a creature so woebegone." He was put to work giving children rides on his saddled back around Regent's Park, a favorite of Queen Victoria's children. Children would pay a fee to feed him currant buns. Jumbo lived for about twenty-five years, spending his life in captivity, first the zoo, later transferred to the circus, due to his fits of grief and rage becoming even more unmanageable as he reached mating age. (Grief and rage over his mother's death? His relentless labor ferrying children? The claustrophobia of his small enclosures?). Scott would also prod and thrash the elephant, to try to tame his aggression, which he deemed adolescent. Jumbo broke his tusks by ramming against the walls of his cage at night, and when they regrew, he would grind them against the stone enclosure, in despair. There were night terrors, calmed only by a bottle of whiskey shared with his human companion and keeper. This repetitive self-mutilating behavior is referred to as stereotypic behavior, repetitive gestures exhibited by humans and other animals in distress, including in the caged conditions of zoo animals, such as also pacing around and around in a circle, which for elephants can accompany a quasi-dance that the filmmaker Chris Marker names "Slon Tango" in a four-minute film, part of his *Bestiaire* series, a long-sustained shot of an elephant in the Ljubljana Zoo ambulating around its enclosure, making seemingly syncopated steps to Stravinsky's "Tango." But Chris Marker's eye here, as usual with his animals, is gentle and compassionate, there is a pathos to the slowness of the lumbering backstep of the Lithuanian soloist. For Tom McCarthy, in his dense, acrobatic *Artforum* blurb, the most important Marker motif is memory—perhaps, he theorizes, the elephant is actually remembering a historical past of a courtship ritual, or perhaps just a dance he's choreographed for the duration of captivity, and he references, as so many inevitably do, the mythical newspaper article that apparently inspired Nabokov to write *Lolita*—the ape in the Jardin des Plantes who picks up a piece of charcoal to execute a sketch of the bars of his cage. Still to this day, zoos sell drawings or paintings made by their animals, who, the gimmick suggests, are really artists, although the labor of their constant work is, as with so many artists, made invisible by their gallerists/keepers. For the elephants picking up a brush, painting eases their anxiety, which is a feature of captivity, but one that can be remedied with a form of occupational therapy, or so the zoo's own literature suggests. At the Cincinnati Zoo, the "brush in trunk" package comes with a custom canvas, with two photographs of your elephant (*your* elephant) creating the art, for the price of only $200, with $30 for shipping across the United States. There is a list, at other zoos, of animals who paint—apes, inheritors of the late chimpanzee artist Congo, whose colorful expressionist paintings are collected by the filmmaker John Waters, but also a variety of other animals including giraffes, sea lions, rhinos, and hippos, as well as lizards, snakes, and penguins.

What am I performing here? Something like a bestiary. A collection—that was the Victorian zoo language. When in 1882 P. T. Barnum purchased Jumbo for his collection, one hundred thousand children wrote to Queen Victoria to protest. But not only was Jumbo's aggression seen as a possible danger, there was also concern that a mature elephant's erections would be too much for a Victorian crowd. He was shipped off to America with Matthew Scott, in a crate that barely fit his six-ton body, plied with alcohol to calm him. He was photographed arriving with his trunk waving out of his crate, promenaded to Madison Square Garden to be exhibited. I am still of an age to remember the Ringling Brothers Circus, before the elephants were retired—in fact I am roughly the age John Berger was when he wrote his treatise on looking at animals at zoos, also finding myself at middle age with young children, taking them to zoos, despite my ambivalence. My aunt would take us, as well as to the popcorn movies, and we would eat pink cotton candy. I remember weeping while watching *Dumbo* in the theater with my aunt, a story of a young elephant, with his ears for flying, who is taken from his mother and forced to be a circus performer, inspired by Jumbo. At the Ringling Brothers Circus, I can remember seeing in the ring, the circle of elephants. Jumbo was only in the circus for three years, making P. T. Barnum millions. Famously he died being struck by a train in Ontario, Canada, while being shuttled by Scott to his boxcar, although there is still a mystery as to the circumstances. Was it an instant death, due to his tusk becoming lodged in his brain, or is there truth to the story Barnum gave the press, that he was trying to save a smaller elephant, Tom Thumb, from the oncoming train? Was he always dying of tuberculosis and Barnum paid off Scott so that he didn't hurry his charge along the tracks? Jumbo's hide was mounted and exhibited for a four-year tour, then sent to Tufts University, where Barnum was a trustee, where it burned in a fire, and his eleven-foot-tall skeleton was donated to the American Museum of Natural History. "If I can't have Jumbo living, I'll have Jumbo dead, and Jumbo dead is worth a small herd of ordinary elephants," Barnum said to *The New York Times*. According to Jumbo's postmortem report, his stomach was revealed to contain "a hat-full of English pennies, gold and silver coins, stones, a bunch of keys, lead seals from railway trucks, trinkets of metal and glass, screws, rivets, pieces of wire, and a police whistle," the souvenirs of a life in captivity, and from snatching coins from the children. An important early memory for the artist Joseph Cornell was seeing Harry Houdini at the Hippodrome with his parents. I don't know this for sure, but I like to think it was in 1918, when he would have been fifteen years old, and Houdini disappeared Jennie the elephant into a huge cabinet (the illusion is difficult to explain, but basically Jennie took her sugar, sauntered into the front of the cabinet, and then twelve men pivoted the cabinet so that when it opened it appeared empty, because of a black interior curtain. This section of the bestiary is beginning to feel like a huge cabinet to fit the elephant. Turn it around and around and eventually all the elephants will disappear.

During the Second World War, a majority of the animal inhabitants of Japan's Ueno Zoo were killed in secret by their keepers, either by starvation, strangulation, or blows or spears, or poison, specifically strychnine, which produces a slow, painful death, first muscular convulsions then ultimately death by asphyxia or exhaustion. But three remaining Indian elephants—John, Tonky, and Wanri—known by children throughout the empire—were starved to death, when the poison did not work, which took up to four weeks, despite repeated efforts by the elephants to perform tricks to get treats. A children's picture book, *Faithful Elephants*, which literally translates to "poor elephants," written by Yukio Tsuchiya and published in Japan in 1951, depicts the army as requesting that the Japanese zoo poison their large animals, because they were worried that they would escape and harm the public in the case of a bomb detonating nearby. Tsuchiya has said she wrote the book so that children would know the grief caused by war. But what really happened in the summer of 1943 is less clear—there are reports that the governor of Tokyo ordered the slaughter of the large animals at the zoo for propaganda reasons, to shock the residents of Tokyo into supporting the realities of war. Besides the elephants, twenty-four residents of the zoo were executed, including bears, lions, a leopard (poisoned), polar bears who couldn't be starved and so were strangled by wire. A memorial service was held for the animals by government officials, attended by the governor himself, as well as hundreds of school children, who were the designated audience. The animals were mourned as martyrs for the country. The animals went to their death so the people would know the inevitability of air attacks. It was a death by honor. In the children's letters originating from all over Japan, they were upset and furious with America and Britain for causing these beloved animals to have to be killed. The proper nationalist feelings were stirred, as so often is the case with a nation's feelings toward the animals they feel they own. See another zoo celebrity, Knut the polar bear in Berlin, satirized so memorably in Yoko Tawada's *Memoirs of a Polar Bear*, his rejection by and orphaning from his also captive mother at birth representing his generational alienation from her maternal past as circus performer and from his grandmother, a Russian émigré writing of her experiences in the minor language, just like Kafka's lecturing animals. Knut the polar bear became the cause célèbre symbol of our climate crisis, the unnatural environment of the zoo a reminder of global warming, superimposed while at the Berlin Zoo by

Annie Leibowitz on the cover of *Vanity Fair* with Leonardo DiCaprio, who was on a glacier lagoon in Iceland. The real Knut died at the age of four having suffered a seizure and drowned with a splash into his pool while people watched. The theater of heartbreak and mourning that unleashed—with fans leaving the stuffed animal versions of him near his cage. He was taxidermied and put on display at the natural history museum, enshrined in a bronze statue, the typical process of mourning for revered zoo animals that also helps to ease the real, hidden, loss for the city, that of touristry and ticket sales. It's not easy to make a successful animal statue, especially of a polar bear. In nineteenth-century Paris one trained to be an animalier, as Rodin did with Antoine-Louis Barye. There is the marble sculpture by François Pompon, assistant to Rodin and Camille Claudel at the Musée d'Orsay. How does one get the fur right, the tones of the white fur the nature writer Barry Lopez began to refuse to photograph and that Tawada imbues with such painterly surrealism. Pompon also eschewed realism and went for the intuitive, essential nature of the polar bear. Colette admired the "thick, mute" paws. After my first zoo report, about the melancholy and strangeness of monkey cages, was published, someone wrote me: "I wonder if that melancholic quality is part of what appeals to children about zoos—they have so few opportunities for indulging their own melancholia, especially girls, so much pressure to have everything unicorns and rainbows." This felt profound to me, especially since this writer is the author of a forthcoming biography of Anne Frank, the iconic melancholic young girl, meditating upon her adolescent feelings, set amidst her attic captivity. I wonder if the zoo is a place where young children can feel these intense feelings of sadness and mortality, including the deep formal mourning for zoo animals that are extinct, or have died in the conditions of their captivity.

Chris Marker's elegiac memory film, *Sans Soleil*, is like a menagerie, occupied by so many animals and their funerals, from a shrine to missing cats to the death of the panda at the Ueno Zoo, most likely the death of Lan Lan in 1979, along with her "groom," Kang Kang, a special gift from China to the people of Japan, who might have delivered the first giant panda born in captivity had she lived one more month. The female narrator, reflecting on a letter that the Marker alter ego Sandor Krasna wrote her, meditates upon the funerals for animals in Japan, with the same chrysanthemums as are customary for the funerals for humans, a day of mourning for all animals that died that year intensified by the panda's death, which was experienced with more grief than when the prime minister died at approximately the same time. Perhaps this day of mourning for the dead panda, and the ritual of weeping, brings about a catharsis as Aristotle describes in his poetics on tragedy. "I've heard this sentence: 'The partition that separates life from death does not appear so thick to us as it does to a Westerner.' What I have read most often in the eyes of people about to die is surprise. What I read right now in the eyes of Japanese children is curiosity, as if they were trying—in order to understand the death of an animal—to stare through the partition." The juxtaposition of daily life and the passage of time in Guinea-Bissau and Tokyo in *Sans Soleil*, first the Japanese children laying flowers at the funerary scene at the Ueno Zoo, then a cinematic gunshot from a B film, seemingly the poachers aiming toward the giraffe in Africa, who first runs around, staggers, then crumples to the ground, the almost ecstatic horror of the spurts of blood flying out. A quick shot of a chrysanthemum flower juxtaposed with the unmourned face of the dead giraffe, being picked at by vultures. Only banality, the ephemerality of time, interests the traveling documentarian Sandor Krasna. "On this trip I've tracked it with the relentlessness of a bounty hunter." So is the giraffe then a metaphor, or some elegiac statement about different attitudes toward animals and mortality, or both? All animals in Chris Marker's films are political, writes Tom McCarthy. There was an outcry at the Copenhagen Zoo, where Marius the baby giraffe was euthanized by a rifle, publicly dissected, then fed to lions. He was healthy but genetically unsuitable for captive breeding programs, apparently. The children didn't cry, newspaper reports read. They were curious and asked questions. During the most recent pandemic, when zoos were closed to the public, there was an ambient paranoia about what might happen to the animals without paying customers, including from one German zoo who threatened that the animals might have to be fed to other animals if they couldn't afford food. The last on the food chain would be their twelve-foot-tall polar bear. This somehow parallels the abovementioned fear about large animals running free during the European world wars. Germany shot many of their large animals in advance of air raids. Those not shot were killed in other ways, such as the elephants at the Berlin Zoo. The London Zoo killed all of their poisonous snakes at the beginning of the Second World War. The Antwerp Zoo killed some of their large animals during both world wars. The hoofed animals slaughtered because of the food shortage. Others froze to death. The Egyptian Temple, housing the giraffes, collapsed. Sebald describes the Antwerp nocturama in the opening pages of *Austerlitz*, his lists of the nocturnal animals also like a bestiary, reminiscent of Borges's imaginary creatures, which Sebald cites throughout his works, including *The Rings of Saturn*. His only lasting memory of that zoo is of a racoon washing a piece of apple over and over again. I wonder if Sebald knew of the tragic story of Rembrandt Bugatti, younger brother of the automobile manufacturer, who would spend days at the Jardin des Plantes, studying the animals he watched there as the subjects for his bronze sculptures, like his walking panther, the beauty of his carved muscles. This was around the same time Rilke was studying his panther at the same Paris zoo for hours, his exhausted vision from the passing bars, at the advice of Rodin, who was known to carry a small carved model of a panther in his pocket for inspiration. It is most likely that the poet and the animalier were together, in front of the panther cage, forming their own imagined bonds with the animal, if the dates line up correctly (1904 for the panther sculpture, between 1902 and 1903 for Rilke's poem). Both found solace from their financial troubles and bouts of depression standing at that zoo, watching the animals. The sculptor volunteered as a paramedic at an Antwerp hospital during the First World War, and would spend his time off at the zoo there, in companionable silence with the animals. After his friends were slaughtered due to food shortages, he himself committed suicide. Which feels like a story that Sebald would have known, or would have liked, but he sadly died before the age of Wikipedia. In *Sans Soleil* the Marker alter ego tells us, through his distanced address, that he has spent his days in front of the TV, "that memory box." For me over the past year it's the laptop. Has it really been a year since I've been to the zoo? My zoo feelings have been memories, usually historical memories that are not mine, from what I've gleaned from reports read online and in books.

• • •

For so long I've abandoned my zoo studies, but still I've remained zoo aware. Back to *Austerlitz*, the cut-out of the gaze of an owl in the Antwerp nocturama resembles Chris Marker's trancelike owl short, "An Owl is an Owl is an Owl," fast cuts of a series of intense owl gazes. The zoo narrative this year in New York City was the Eurasian eagle-owl Flaco, who escaped his enclosure at the Central Park Zoo when someone cut his stainless-steel netting. He lasted nine months eating rats and pigeons while being spotted on Manhattan high rises and in the park. There was a debate about his survival in the wild, whether he should be captured again, a narrative of captivity only complicated when he died from injuries colliding into a building, and was found with high levels of rat poison in his system as well a severe affliction of pigeon herpes (please ignore the comments about this, that assume Flaco was doing something else with the pigeons, other than eating them, to get herpes). I only viewed the crowded memorial service at Central Park online, with crayoned drawings of the owl, signs proclaiming "Fly Free Flaco!" even in death. I am reminded of the funerals for birds my children would hold in Prospect Park, during summer camp, although not aware the birds have most likely died in such number because of rat poison, feral cats, or perhaps the intense heat. Children are instructed into the lives of animals usually through the death of insects, although they are not as aware that those are disappearing as well. The history of the zoo is now also footnoted with its relationship to natural and manmade disaster. It was only this spring that I became aware that our local zoo had been closed since the flooding last September because of damage to the electrical grid. Twenty-five feet of water in the basement. None of the four hundred animals apparently were harmed and they got to stay in their habitats. Were those inside just in the dark, without electricity? The person cutting my hair, who has two children the same age as mine, informed me of the closure. How was I not aware? We had withdrawn into our private family unit, alienated from the natural world, locked into a pattern of work and school, just as John Berger predicted. Again, I was hit with that zoo feeling that began all this, the feeling of an absence of years from the zoo, the strange warp of my memories. As I write this it's now Memorial Day weekend. The zoo is opening up again. Look, there are new baby baboons. Have you been porcu-pining for us, since you've been away? Thus concludes my reports on the zoo, two years after my first report was written, three years after my lectures ended.

MY KAFKA

SYSTEM

THE MISSING PERSON

BACHELOR JOURNEY

In July 1908, a twenty-five-year-old Franz Kafka quit his post at Assicurazioni Generali with a medical note claiming he was suffering from "nervousness" and something potentially complicated having to do with his heart. This despite passing the medical examination when hired less than a year before (height: 5'11"; weight: 134 pounds; nutritional status: "moderately weak," digestion and appetite surprisingly normal; an "even," "buttery yellow" urine stream). Now a trainee at the Workers' Accident Insurance Institute, he had a certain amount of vacation every year (two weeks, taken in late summer or early fall, which he stretched to three with a medical note about his nervous exhaustion). He was lucky—a six-hour position, no second shift. For a Jew to have found, no less. He began the first of his holidays with the Brod brothers, Max and Otto, in northern Italy (the air show at Brescia, the waters at Riva). The next trip they took was to Paris, in the fall of 1910. The plan was to stay for three weeks, though he would only last for one.

THE SPECIFIC NATURE OF HIS MISERY

The earliest extant Kafka diaries we have are from this period, when he used his time off to travel for pleasure. Now that he had time, he could write—or, really, complain in writing about not having enough time to write. This is when the young Kafka begins to philosophize his writer's block. Many of these entries are from Sundays, when he had to contend with the chaotic domestic atmosphere of the Kafka household. There is a compressed anxiety to these entries. Reading the early diaries, it's clear that Kafka felt incapable of writing the kind of sentence he desired. "I write this very decidedly out of despair over my body and over a future with this body," he writes on one of the first pages, a manifesto that catalyzes his practice.

FLAUBERT OR PORTRAIT

Before that first trip to Paris, Kafka and the Brod brothers studied French, mainly to read Flaubert's *Sentimental Education* in its original language. There was little Kafka loved as much as that book. Max Brod soon declared *Sentimental Education* his favorite book as well, hanging a portrait of Flaubert over his desk. Kafka saw himself as the spiritual son of Flaubert.

Like Kafka, Flaubert lived and worked in his familial home. In 1842, Flaubert was a failure as a law student, a mess of nerves and migraines, miserable in Paris, habituating brothels instead of lectures. All this Flaubert channeled into his character Frédéric, the bored and voluptuous law student. I envision Flaubert's dandy Frédéric (in pressed coat and patent-leather boots) next to that image of Kafka as a young law student himself, a photograph made sometime in 1906 and often reproduced in biographies—English bowler, frock coat, stiff collar. A stiffness or stillness to Kafka's gaze here, like in so many photographs from the turn of the twentieth century. He is holding a look, somewhat awkwardly, most likely at the photographer's insistence. Biographers often interpret this gaze as a melancholy one, reading into it his later tales of alienation. There's a mystery to this photograph of Kafka before he became Kafka. It is difficult to know what he is thinking here. I don't think he looks melancholy. If anything, there's a wryness to his expression, although it's rather blank. What did Kafka see? What is behind his gaze? This is what I'm searching for.

TOURIST

The first time he was in Paris, Kafka did not keep a travel diary. The three young men on holiday most likely behaved as typical male tourists: they went to the postcard sites, to the cabarets, to the night cafés, to the theater, the Louvre. Kafka went alone to the horse races. There were no specific traces of Flaubert's haunts to follow. Perhaps they would have wished to find Monsieur Arnoux's art shop on the Boulevard Montmartre, but it would not have been there.

TRAFFIC

In his unfinished story "Wedding Preparations in the Country," Kafka attempted to copy the spirit of the early passage on Parisian traffic in *Sentimental Education*, a paragraph that must have resonated with him as he first encountered the streets of Paris. The paragraph itself is a form of traffic. At first the phrases and sentences circulate like the women lolling in their barouches, the flow and swarm of bodies and vehicles in the city, the sentences gaining movement and momentum. While Frédéric takes in the scene, more and more carriages appear, rubbing against each other, mane against mane, lamp against lamp, while he imagines the face of his beloved Madame Arnoux appearing in one of the broughams. Everything is bottlenecked and cramped, until a scattering of the carriages that is like a sexual release. The traffic disperses as the sun goes down, the gas lamps burning.

BOILS

Kafka's Paris was louder and faster, dirtier and more clogged, than Flaubert's. Kafka was fascinated and horrified by the noise of the métro. He arrived in Paris with a sprained toe and a breakout of furunculosis—pus-filled bumps—all over his back. He kept on having to wrap his torso tightly so as to cover the wounds. As he roamed endlessly through Montmartre, up the grand boulevards, the bandages would loosen, and he would give up and return to his hotel. After a week of constant pain and itching, he decided to go home to Prague and tend to his malady. In three postcards to the brothers Brod sent to their hotel in Paris (a reversal of a postcard's purpose), he performs a quippy hysteria. "Dear Max, I arrived safely and only because I am regarded as an improbable phenomenon by everyone I am very pale. —The pleasure of shouting at the doctor was denied to me by a little fainting spell, which forced me onto his couch and during which—it was peculiar—I felt myself so very much a girl that I attempted to put my girl's skirt in order with my fingers. For the rest, the doctor declared that he was horrified by my appearance from the rear, the 5 new abscesses are no longer so important since a skin eruption has appeared that is worse than all abscesses, requires a long time to heal, and produces and will produce the actual pain." He confesses in the next postcard that he suspects this more recent eruption was the eruption of the city of Paris onto his body, its sidewalks running through him, his body a bumpy, inflamed map. At home in Prague, he must sit still in his plaster cast, which is unbearable, and he dreams at night of Paris traffic.

DREAM

In the third postcard, he writes of a dream of sleeping in a large house populated by such traffic. How sleep hung around his dream like scaffolding around a Parisian building. "I had been lodged for sleeping in a large house that consisted of nothing except Paris horse cabs, automobiles, omnibuses, etc. which had nothing better to do than drive close beside each other, past each other, over each other, and under each other and there was no talk or thought of anything but bus fares, connections, transfers, tips, direction Pereire, counterfeit currency, etc." Reading this last unwinding passage, I am reminded of the snapshots of dread and anxiety in Rainer Maria Rilke's *The Notebooks of Malte Laurids Brigge*, which was published sometime in 1910. Kafka could easily have picked up his fellow Prague writer's novel of fragments in a Paris bookshop; perhaps he even read it on the train home, and this somehow infected his prose, which after this first Paris trip begins to grow denser and more complicated as he attempts to document what he witnesses, much like how Rilke's Malte meditates upon the shock and nervous energy of Paris in 1902. There's a striking parallel between both Kafka's Paris writing and the opening of Rilke's work, with Malte kept awake in his bed by noise and shadows, navigating a sleepless night: "To think that I cannot give up sleeping with the window open. Electric street-cars rage ringing through my room. Automobiles run their way over me. A door slams." Then again, this could simply be a form of sympathetic plagiarism, a twinning of how this city infects the writer and their literature.

MEDICAL MUSEUM

Kafka returned home so as not to inconvenience the Brod brothers, who were continuing on their

Flaubert pilgrimage to his birthplace in Rouen, their rail trip mimicking in reverse Flaubert's occasional trips to the city to see Louise Colet, poet and mistress. The house where Flaubert was born is now a museum of medical history, in honor of Flaubert's father, the chief surgeon of the Hôtel-Dieu, as Flaubert's boyhood home housed his father's medical practice, but also serves as a shrine to the novelist who wrote all of his works there. If Kafka had been able to make the trip, perhaps he would have written of staring meditatively at the stuffed parrot from Flaubert's story "Un coeur simple," which Flaubert kept on his desk while writing. Besides Loulou, the stuffed parrot, the biggest draw to this small museum of mostly medical curios is the hand-sewn leather birthing mannequin from the eighteenth century, an instructive model for midwives, housed in a room dedicated to the dangers of childbirth in that century, or so say the reviewers on Tripadvisor. I think again to the opening pages of Rilke's *The Notebooks of Malte Laurids Brigge*, Malte staring at the grotesquerie waiting outside a Paris hospital, his fascination with pregnant women, the death he sees within them.

• • •

A SECOND LIFE

Although Kafka didn't keep a diary on that first trip to Paris, the experience leaches into his later notes, and over time he romanticizes this disastrous failure of a trip. He knows he'll return. On February 21, 1911, he writes, "My life here is just as if I were quite certain of a second life, in the same way, for example, I got over the pain of my unsuccessful visit to Paris with the thought that I would try to go there again very soon. With this, the sight of the sharply divided light and shadows on the pavement of the street." Toward the end of 1910, upon returning from this trip, Kafka begins to inhabit his diary regularly. He returns to the imagery of Paris traffic as a metaphor for writer's block. When he sits down at his desk, he feels "no better than someone who falls and breaks both legs in the middle of the traffic of the Place de l'Opéra" with carriages rushing "from all directions in all directions." And yet, "that man's pain keeps better order than the police, it closes his eyes and empties the Place and the streets without the carriages having to turn about. The great commotion hurts him, for he is really an obstruction to traffic, but the emptiness is no less sad, for it unshackles his real pain." The emptiness here is the emptiness of the blank page. In these entries there is also a renewed commitment to writing, a desire to devote all of his available energies to the act of literature, which includes his diary, a form of documentation and punctuation as to whether he was able to write that day. At ten o'clock at night on November 10, he writes that he will not let himself be tired, he will "jump into my story even though it should cut my face to pieces." The nocturnal rhythm of writing becomes a second shift of the day, when he refuses sleep in order to write.

AVIARY

During the day his room was the center of the entire Kafka apartment at Niklasstrasse 36, fourth floor, where he lived with his parents, his three sisters, and a maid. Since he was situated between his parents' bedroom and the main living area, in the morning he was routinely subject to whispering, yawning, the creaking bed of his parents, doors slamming, his father bursting through, robe trailing, the boom of his voice, Has my hat been cleaned yet? In a piece titled "Great Noise," Kafka describes this typical Sunday family disorder, his attempts to work, his slithering like a snake into the living room to beg his sisters and their governess to please be quiet. Kafka had his own room, unlike his three sisters who crowded into one, yet biographers still sympathetically note how cold and cramped it was. Kafka was mordantly sensitive to noise. As accompaniment to everything else, there was the constant chirping of the canaries. At night in the Kafka household, once everyone else was asleep, Kafka would go into the living room, place a cover over the cage, a blanket on his lap, and continue filling up another of his notebooks. This was the domestic sphere that Kafka was trying to escape through his bachelor journeys. He worked at home, and his work was of the home, the enclosed and often claustrophobic domestic space. Traveling was a way to disappear, and also to escape his family, especially his father. I want to think of this paragraph like a cage or an aviary, enclosing Kafka's desire to escape.

FATHER

In *K.*, his book on Kafka, Roberto Calasso writes of the transformation of photographs of the patriarch Hermann Kafka, before and after his son's death at forty from tuberculosis. In earlier photographs, Hermann, the son of a butcher, looks like a boxer—a robust man with a thick neck and twirly mustache—even though he is dressed dapperly in a formal suit and bow tie, as befitting the owner of a wholesale fancy-goods store. It is easy to imagine him brutalizing his son with his sheer presence, sucking all the energy out of a room. In a photograph of Kafka's parents after their son's early death, Hermann, wearing a three-piece suit, now looks much older. He has shrunk to half his former size. The son in his lifetime shrinking before his father's oppressiveness, and then afterward, the father becoming more anemic and frail, mirroring his son after death. Kafka the son is often thought of as the sickly one, but his father dramatized his health as well. You weren't supposed to excite him because of his heart condition, and like the rest of the family, he vacationed separately at various sanatoriums. In 1911, the night before he was to leave with Max Brod on their trip through the continent, Kafka recorded in his diary that his father was quite ill—suffering from insomnia because of anxiety over his business, which had exacerbated his illness. Up all night vomiting. Pacing back and forth with a wet cloth on his heart, loudly sighing.

TRAVEL DIARY

They departed Prague by rail at noon on August 28, 1911. Onward to Italy through Switzerland. The plan was for the two friends to individually keep travel diaries and later collaborate on turning their notes into a satirical travelogue they would title *Richard and Samuel: A Brief Journey through Central European Regions*. The idea behind these travel diaries—to describe not only the trip but also their feelings toward each other along the way—was, Kafka writes (rather punchily), "a poor one." Later, over the months they met at Brod's house on Sundays to work on this book, Kafka became so frustrated that he wondered in his diary whether he should keep yet another private notebook, one he would not share with Brod, devoted to complaints about this project and their friendship. The opening of this travel diary chronicles in some detail the first leg of the trip, on their way to Munich. Later the two would fictionalize their encounter with a young woman, Alice R., with whom they flirt on the train and then later share a quick and giggling evening taxicab through Munich, in the first and only chapter of *Richard and Samuel*, titled "The First Long Train

Journey Prague–Zurich." It's telling how quickly Kafka wrote the first passage in his travel diary (probably worked on it over a day), and then how many months it took to turn it into something else, how torturous this process felt. How slow it can be, any attempt to make fiction out of the present. It is clear reading both his present-tense travel diaries and his more layered memories written at the end of the trip that Kafka viewed his vacation as a writing holiday, for paying attention and taking notes. While at a table outside of the cathedral in Milan, he writes that it is "inexcusable to travel—or even live—without taking notes. The deathly feeling of the monotonous passing of the days is made impossible."

TRAIN

The notes he takes from the train are dashed-off, hyphenated bursts, like the stop and start of passing through stations. Later, in the reading room at the sanatorium in Zurich, going through his notes, he meditates that there is a calmer, more pastoral mode of thought in Goethe's travel diaries because of the slowness of the horse-drawn mail coach. The aphoristic quality of Kafka's travel diary. On his way to

Paris, he writes, "I didn't know whether I was sleepy or not, and the question bothered me all morning on the train. Don't mistake the nursemaids for French governesses of German children." When Brod remembered their abbreviated stay in Milan, a city he detested, he thought of a train model he saw there in a toy store window. A model also for their collaboration—circling around and around, going nowhere.

SWIMMING

Look closely at the picture postcards Kafka sent home to his sisters Ottla and Valli, at the vast blue of the lakes surrounded by mountains, and you can see the two friends of differing heights bobbing gently in the water. Such an awful, abnormal heat wave, the summer of 1911. They embraced with relief in the water at Lake Maggiore in Stresa. The two of them believed they must swim in a body of water to establish a physical connection with, and thus possession of, a landscape. Before his trip, Kafka records that although he has failed to write a word all summer, he has spent much time swimming, mostly at the Civilian Swimming Pool in Prague, and in doing so has conquered something of his despair and disgust over his frailty. Finally, he stopped being ashamed of his body in the swimming pools in Prague, Königssee, and Czernowitz.

CONSTIPATION

His worry over his poor digestion and his health or relative fitness was a labor he undertook during the day that almost matched the ardency of his nighttime literary investigations. The attempt to relieve his constipation marks a rhythm in the diaries. Having just returned from his three weeks traveling, he records that a friend recommended a more natural laxative, a powdered seaweed that swells up the bowels. Kafka loved to list food, as in a letter to Max Brod from the Swiss sanatorium in the final, solo, doctor-prescribed leg of his trip. Rather than draft the story Brod instructed him to work on, he writes about his sluggish digestion and lists his meals: mashed potatoes, applesauce, vegetable and fruit juices, whole-grain breads, omelets, puddings, and above all nuts. His biographer Reiner Stach notes Hermann's irritation at his only son's daily breakfast (yogurt, chestnuts, dates, figs, grapes, almonds, raisins, berries, whole-grain bread, and oranges). Kafka's travel diaries are often punctuated by what he ate. The butter served at breakfast at the temperance restaurant in Zurich "like egg yolk." In Lucerne: pea soup with sago, baked potato, beans, lemon crème. At a café at twilight in Paris: "I ordered a yogurt, then another."

FRUIT

"Fruit," he notes in Switzerland. In Zurich Kafka is happy to be out of his room, though he would have liked to have had some fruit. In Italy suddenly: "No fruit." He eats apple strudels in Milan and desires better pastries in Paris. Orange sodas and sherbets. He keeps on drinking fizzy, sugary beverages, even though they bother his stomach. It is always unbearably hot out. In Milan, his passion for iced drinks punishes him: he drinks one grenadine and two aranciatas in the theater, one in the bar on the Corso Vittorio Emanuele, one sherbet in the coffeehouse in the Galleria, one French Thierry mineral water. Brod is horrified by Kafka's constant consumption of fruit and iced drinks in sultry (and, to Brod, awful) Milan. Brod wants to heed the warnings not to eat fruits or vegetables. He is intensely phobic because of the news abroad, leaked in the German newspapers, about the Italian government covering up the cholera epidemic. In the years since, it has been speculated that sixteen thousand people died of cholera in Italy in 1911—perhaps 2,600 people between May and September in Naples alone. Thomas Mann was in Italy that same summer, and he sets *Death in Venice* amid this same sweltering paranoia: "Obsessed with obtaining reliable news about the status and progress of the disease, he went to the city's cafés and plowed through all the German newspapers, which had been missing from the hotel lobby during the past few days." It is the temptation of a strawberry that finally kills Mann's Gustav von Aschenbach, a cause of death modeled on Gustav Mahler, who died just that May in Vienna. It's amusing that the usually hypochondriacal Kafka is so flippant about cholera, unlike Brod, hysterically applying Vaseline to his mosquito bites. They are irritated with each other over these twenty-four hours in Milan, bickering constantly. Kafka convinces Brod to climb to the top of the cathedral in ninety-five-degree heat, and yet he later concedes that the cathedral, with all its spires, was "a little tiresome." Outside of the shopping arcade with the glass domes at Cathedral Square, Brod begs Kafka to promise that if he dies, he will be administered a lethal heart injection, like Mahler had requested for himself, to make sure he is really dead. They decide to return to Paris, despite the disaster of the previous year, where Kafka writes in his travel diary of yearning to go about the side streets looking for fruit.

BROTHEL

Then there is the cubist centerpiece of fruit at the bottom of *Les Demoiselles d'Avignon*, the painting Picasso worked on for years and that he thought of as a "philosophical brothel." It's a strange little gesture, like a sneer or tribute to mannered composition (here you are, Cézanne). Kafka's description of the prostitutes in Milan (disdain) versus the next passage on fizzy drinks (delight). Everything feels paradoxical. "The girls spoke their French like virgins. Milanese beer smells like beer, tastes like wine." Kafka sketches quick portraits of the women in a way that also calls to mind Degas's brothel monotypes, especially the one with the four faceless, naked women, seated, legs akimbo, arms crossed, the focus on the black triangles of their bushes. A long, winding description that reads like a sketch for one of the later novels—a seated girl, her belly "spread shapelessly over and between her outspread legs under her transparent dress." He is fascinated by the "round, talkative, and devoted knees" of a Frenchwoman, her talent for thrusting money into her stocking. He fixates on an old man's hands on her knee. A sinister Spanish woman with a sinister Spanish face stands by the door, body stretched in a sheath of "prophylactic silk." At home, "it was with the German bordello girls that one lost a sense of one's nationality for a moment, here it was with the French girls." The three-quarter circle in which the unengaged girls stood around the two visitors, crowded together closely, drawing themselves up in certain postures, like the five women of *Les Demoiselles d'Avignon*. Picasso owned eleven of the fifty or so extant Degas monotypes. The word *bordel* is associated with chaos. Perhaps this essay (or is it a story?) reads like a bordello, all these figures crowded together.

DREAM

Months after this Paris trip, Kafka dreams of walking through a row of houses to a brothel, a gigantic row of rooms without doors, rooms with dirty rumpled beds. In the dream, there are two women on the floor, Max Brod is with one, Kafka with the other. He runs his fingers across the woman's legs and presses her thighs in a regular rhythm. "My pleasure in this was so great that I wondered that for this entertainment, which really after all was the most beautiful kind, one still had to pay nothing," he writes. The woman sits up, then turns her back to him. To his "horror," it was "covered with large sealing-wax-red circles with paling edges, and red splashes scattered among them." He begins pressing his thumb all over into these spots, noticing too that there are "little red particles—as though from a crumbled seal" on his fingers as well. Suddenly, he observes Brod on the floor eating a rather chunky potato soup.

FIGURE

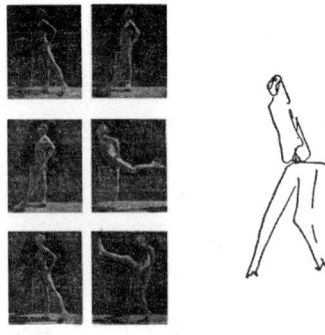 

In his published conversations with Kafka, Gustav Janouch recalls seeing an exhibition with Kafka featuring Picasso's exuberant, pink-fleshed giantesses with oversized feet. Janouch remarks that Picasso was a "willful distortionist," to which Kafka apparently replies, "He only registers the deformities which have not yet penetrated our consciousness." In his diaries, and later, the literary works, Kafka trains a fragmenting gaze on women's faces and bodies especially. The figurative doodles in Kafka's diaries, a few of which are printed in the English translation, look like sketchy embodiments of the photographs from Jørgen Peter Müller's *My System*, the 1904 book of exercises by the Danish gymnast that Kafka followed religiously, performing naked calisthenics in front of his open window, even in winter. Back in Prague, having returned from the second trip to Paris, he continues writing sketches of his brothel visits in his diary. Girls "dressed like the marionettes for children's theatres that are sold in the Christmas market, i.e. with ruching and gold stuck on and loosely sewn so that one can rip them with one pull and they then fall apart in one's fingers." A "landlady with the pale blonde hair," her "sharply slanting nose . . . in some sort of geometric relation to the sagging breasts and the stiffly held belly." Entries at the theater in Milan that conjure the black-shadowed realism of Manet. "Tall, vigorous actor with delicately painted nostrils; the black of the nostrils continued to stand out even when the outline of his upturned face was lost in the light. Girl with a long slender neck ran off-stage with short steps and rigid elbows—you could guess at the high heels that went with the long neck. . . . Nose and mouth of a girl shadowed by her painted eyes. Man in a box opened his mouth when he laughed until a gold molar became visible, then kept it open like that for a while." Kafka notices what everyone's wearing at the theater—always in his diaries an attention to clothes. In a Prague entry, he observes a large button on a dress, paired with American boots, and wishes he could create something as beautiful in writing as this mere button. But especially he observes the faces of women in uncomfortable detail, a surgical gaze he later trains on the feminine figures in his fiction. He is obsessed with Semitic features. He observes that a young Italian woman's "otherwise Jewish face became non-Jewish in profile." He writes an entire paragraph in an extreme close-up about the way she stands up and leans forward. She is reading a paperback detective story that her brother had been begging to read. Her father has a "hooked nose," but hers, being gently curved, is "more Jewish." Women especially have masks in Kafka's work. In his diary a year later, after meeting his future fiancée Felice Bauer in the Brod living room: "Bony, empty face that wore its emptiness openly . . . Almost broken nose."

PHOTOGRAPH

While still a young law student, Kafka was crazy about a twenty-one-year-old wine-bar hostess who went by the nickname Hansi. (She in turn called him Franzi.) He often visited her in her room, where she spent entire days in bed, a detail he stores away for the character based on her in *The Trial*. She is actually in the other half of the photograph of Kafka the dandy, posing with a dog between them. They are both petting the dog, a panting German shepherd. Hansi wears a pillbox hat suspended over an elaborate braided coiffure, a smart buttoned suit and tie (her work uniform, perhaps). She is slightly out of focus. It is difficult to know whether her smile is of a professional variety, or something more intimate. Maybe she is laughing. In the complete portrait, Kafka looks rather debonair, even mischievous. In most photographs published in biographies and circulated online, Hansi and the dog have been cropped out entirely. In some versions, Kafka's body has also been cropped, just a floating pale head with a bowler hat. In others, he is shown with the dog, absent Hansi. That movement to make this photograph one of solitude, what does it say? Do we desire our Kafka unhappy and alone?

In the complete portrait, their hands are on the dog, perhaps to keep him from lunging at the photographer. Picasso originally intended to put a dog in his philosophical brothel painting—he did numerous sketches of dogs for the work. In one, a dog humps the leg of a male visitor, often referred to as the medical student, who is ultimately omitted from the final painting. There are several sketches in which the dog is nursing puppies. The blurriness of the dog in this portrait reminds me of one of Francis Bacon's ghostly dog paintings, inspired by the nineteenth-century photographic studies of human and animal movement by Eadweard Muybridge, which Bacon kept as references in the living ruin of his studio. Muybridge stills motion in multiple frames, which Bacon enfolds in a single image. Muybridge's most absurd study is of a naked woman feeding a dog, as seen from three angles, which I now associate, in my mind, with Hansi.

STATUARY

The Prague wine bar where Hansi was a hostess was named the Trocadero, and shares its name with the Palais du Trocadéro in Paris, built for the 1878 World's Fair. Kafka was impressed by this colossus of Moorish design when he visited Paris, or perhaps he felt drawn to the site because it reminded him of his favorite wine bar back home. Within the gardens of the old palace were two large statues, a rhinoceros and an elephant, now in front of the Musée d'Orsay. At some point in the nineteenth century, the head

of the Statue of Liberty was also exhibited in those same gardens. There's something uncanny about photographs of such an iconic monument without a torso, unable to raise her phantom arm, her large head dwarfing the park benches and trees, like Kafka's opening image of the Statue of Liberty holding a sword instead of a flame in his unfinished novel *Amerika*. Picasso used to frequent the Musée d'Ethnographie du Trocadéro, located within the old palace, where he first discovered the African Fang masks that partially inspired his *Les Demoiselles d'Avignon*. Photos of the museum show a cluttered space, like a junk shop, crowded with statues of hybrid animal-human figures. When Picasso first stepped inside, he wanted to leave immediately, the smell of dampness and rot stuck in his throat. When thinking of W. G. Sebald's story about Kafka in *Vertigo*, the postcards and photographs cluttering the page, it too feels like a junk shop. The internet, repository of old and displaced images, is another sort of junk shop. I wonder why I'm trying to make sense of this detritus.

HEAD

On September 7, 1911, the night before Kafka and Brod arrived in Paris, the poet Guillaume Apollinaire was arrested under suspicion of stealing the *Mona Lisa*. His friend Picasso was also detained. The painting had been stolen two weeks before, on August 21. A week after the painting was stolen, a Belgian, Géry Pieret, who had worked as a kind of secretary to Apollinaire, wrote an anonymous letter to *Paris-Journal* confessing to stealing an ancient Iberian statuette from the Louvre, bragging about the museum's lax security. Several years earlier Pieret had sold Picasso two such ancient Iberian stone heads—a female and male head, even though he only wanted the female head. (The elongated ears and fixed oval eyes of the two central figures in his philosophical brothel painting were inspired by these heads.) Picasso and Apollinaire became paranoid that they would be accused of harboring an art thief and conspiring in an art-trafficking ring, and initially planned to flee. They then decided to pack up the statues in a suitcase, wait until midnight, and throw them in the Seine when no one was looking, a madcap plan also aborted. Finally Apollinaire took the sculptures to *Paris-Journal*'s offices so that they could be anonymously returned to the Louvre, although by then Picasso just wanted to keep them. By that evening, Apollinaire was in jail, accused of being the chief of an international gang seeking to despoil the museums of France. He was strip-searched and incarcerated for several days inside La Santé, the Paris prison, and kept in solitary confinement. The prison registry referred to him as Apollinaris Kostrowitsky, his Polish name, prisoner 216. Picasso was also arrested, but immediately released. On September 12, Apollinaire was brought before the judge to be interrogated. That morning, a plainclothes policeman went to serve a terrified Picasso with a summons to appear. Various accounts depict a collapse in the courtroom—a hysterical Apollinaire standing before the magistrate, confessing to anything the authorities wanted. Apparently Picasso, also a wreck in front of his handcuffed friend, denied even knowing him. For a long time afterward, Picasso was convinced he was being followed by police and only went out at night in a taxi, switching cars several times to throw off the tail. Apollinaire was also haunted by his interrogation and imprisonment. Some accounts suggest he volunteered for the French Army during the First World War in order to erase somehow the stigma of the unsavory foreigner. As I stare at a photograph of the stolen female stone head with its plaited braid, I keep returning to the photograph of Hansi the waitress, her elaborate braided hairstyle. Their uncanny likeness.

THE MONA LISA IS MISSING!

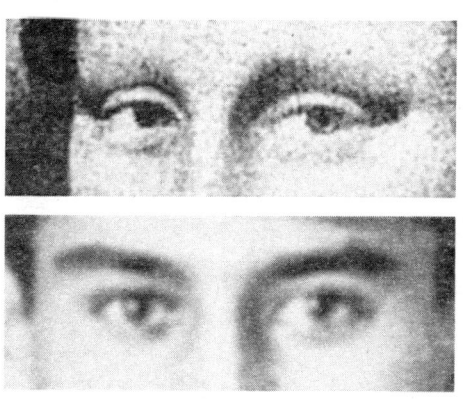

On his second trip to Paris, young Kafka visited the Louvre weeks after the *Mona Lisa* was stolen. When I first read this detail, I imagined him standing meditatively in front of a blank space, staring at the painting's absence, at the spare poetry of the four remaining hooks. But recalling this Louvre visit later in his diary, he focuses on the spectacle of the crowd in the Salon Carré, "the excitement and the knots of the people, as if the *Mona Lisa* had just been stolen." The *Mona Lisa*, after all, only really became the *Mona Lisa* once she was stolen. Her mysterious expression and sedately folded hands multiplied on advertisements, candy boxes, postcards. That night, Kafka and Brod stood in line at the Omnia Pathé to see the five-minute film *Nick Winter and the Theft of the Mona Lisa*, in which the thief returns because he took the wrong painting—he takes Velázquez's *Infanta Margarita* instead. Is Kafka standing in front of the blank space that different than what it's like to stand in the crowds in front of the *Mona Lisa* now? Is it possible to stand in front of that work and really see anything? Is this perhaps part of the allure—the mystery and blankness of her face? I realize writing this that Kafka too is someone I project my thinking and desires onto.

LOUVRE

It's not an easy task to reconstruct what artworks Kafka refers to in the brief list he makes while at the Louvre. I spend weeks puzzling over his notation "Velázquez: Portrait de Philippe IV roi d'Espagne 1599–1600," finally discerning that the Louvre once owned a copy of a painting once attributed to Velázquez—*Portrait of Philip IV in Hunting Costume*—but which is now attributed to Juan Bautista Martínez del Mazo, the Spaniard's assistant and son-in-law. The original and better-known *Philip IV in Hunting Dress* is at the Prado in Madrid. You can tell the difference between the nearly identical fishy-faced, twirly-mustached Philip IVs, both posed with guns and dogs at their feet, by the fact that the king holds his cap in the copy and wears it in the original. Mazo's portrait inspired Manet when he was a copyist at the Louvre for his own etching of *Philip IV in Hunting Costume*. I have no idea why Kafka jotted down these titles in his diary. All I can do is follow the dogs on the edges of certain paintings he writes down. The dog at Philip's side, signaling nobility, is a mastiff much like the sleepy canine in Velázquez's *Las Meninas*. The dog playing in the foreground in

Rubens's *The Kermesse*, a bawdy village wedding scene I imbue with a weird and layered Kafka physicality, inspired by Flaubert. But am I trying to see a Kafka gaze where there is none?

HAND

For his *Portrait of Madame Brunet*, often referred to as the French *Mona Lisa*, Manet imitates the leather glove of Velázquez as well as the pose, the distant landscape. Hermann Kafka's fancy-goods store sold gloves, along with haberdashery, parasols, umbrellas, walking sticks, silk handkerchiefs, silk ribbons, scarves, lace, buttons, slippers, fans, jewelry, and elegant decorative objects and knickknacks made of cast iron, bronze, zinc, silver, leather, wood, ivory, glass, and lead. In *Sentimental Education*, there are numerous descriptions of Frédéric's gloves, "for the gloves that he had ordered were of beaver, whereas the right kind for a funeral were floss-silk." Kafka wrote happily to a friend that he didn't need gloves anymore when outside in the cold air, so toughened had he become by the Müller technique. The clinical horror of illustrated cut-off fingers accompanying Kafka's technical essay from 1910, "Measures for Preventing Accidents from Wood-Planing Machines." In his diary, Kafka quotes from an old notebook: "Now, in the evening, after having studied since six o'clock in the morning, I noticed that my left hand had already for some time been sympathetically clasping my right hand by the fingers."

SENTENCES

All that fall in 1911, Kafka goes over to Max Brod's to work on the travel diary. The writing is going badly in several ways. Often he writes of his imperfect sentences as being full of holes, like spatial things "into which one could stick both hands; one sentence sounds high, one sentence sounds low . . . one sentence rubs against another like the tongue against a hollow or false tooth; one sentence comes marching up with so rough a start that the entire story falls into sulky amazement." It causes him physical pain to listen to Brod read from a story of his at a friend's house. Kafka rationalizes that this is because he doesn't have the time and quiet to draw out all of the great force and possibilities of his talent, in which, despite his doubts, he maintains his faith. "I finish nothing because I have no time and it presses within me," he writes. This will become a refrain over the next two years ("Wrote nothing today . . . Nothing.") He longs to write a story that is large and whole, well shaped, healthy, and then he will never attempt to disavow this piece of writing.

SLEEPLESSNESS

Upon his return from traveling, Kafka experiences a period of insomnia, which he ascribes to his renewed commitment to writing: "No matter how little and how badly I write, I am still made sensitive by these minor shocks, feel, especially toward evening and even more in the morning, the approaching, the imminent possibility of great moments." He falls asleep, wakes up an hour later. It will take one year for him to feel what he has longed for, the full force of his language. His ecstasy once he has conquered time, staying up all night writing. He writes the story "The Judgment" in one sitting, eight straight hours overnight, in September 1912, one year after his Paris trip. His legs grow so stiff that, come morning, he can't pull them out from under the desk. The fearful strain and joy he experiences then.

THE MAN WHO DISAPPEARED

Around this time—along with complaints about the asbestos factory he now must manage, the tensions this causes with his family, his regular job, and Felice—Kafka worries constantly about how much time the publishing of his first small book of stories, *Meditation*, has drained from his literary potential. When confronted with the reality of publishing his writing, he feels panicked about how little has accumulated in his notebooks. The artifice, he vents to himself, of trying to prepare a text for publication, when what he desires is a new prose, to let a work take shape unforced. He doesn't tell his new publishers this, but for a while now he's been thinking about a novel, which he titles *The Man Who Disappeared* or *The Missing Person*, set in the America he has never visited. He doesn't tell his publishers this because they would have wanted the novel before anything else. Kafka wants to keep the novel hidden, a dream, like the dream he had several years earlier of two brothers, one who went to America and the other who was locked up in a European prison. Thinking of Kafka's yearning for this potential novel, was there any book he could have written that would have fulfilled his desires? Or was his longing toward literature something more impossible, or infinite?

INSEKT OR LARGE VERMINOUS THING

Around dusk one evening in March, I went out back to the small garage and switched on my small square of artificial light at my desk, my window in which I now mostly speak to the outside world, in order to give a lecture on Franz Kafka's story *The Metamorphosis*. I was not feeling well, in fact I had occasional spasms in my abdomen, perhaps a bladder infection, and I was exhausted and run-down, but still I had prepared as best as I could to give the lecture. I had spent the previous day, when I was not teaching, on the couch where I spend most of my time, taking pleasure in slowly rereading the story, hunched over my laptop, trying to figure out how to break it up into sections, while also nursing the small child, who has taken to, almost gleefully, stomping on my abdomen with her bare feet while we are lying down. The bladder infection, if that's what it is, for the pain often travels mysteriously through my body, other times an ache in my breast, or a soreness in my hip, has been most likely caused by having to urinate while the baby sleeps on me, and I continue in this way, so as to squeeze any time available for more work, so as not to wake her. This also happens during the hours I am teaching class and in conference with students, almost all in my domestic space when I am also taking care of the child, sometimes plural, children, when my eldest is home from kindergarten, and throughout these labors rarely do I ever take a break to relieve my own body, and now what's happened is I have the urge all the time, and very little comes out. Sometimes lately this body feels so deconstructed that I'm unsure how even to describe it, or assemble it again, in order to move about the world, like a piece of wobbly furniture where all of the instructions are in a foreign language. If it was at all appropriate to speak of my own body during the lecture, even more disembodied through the screen, this might have been a fitting entry point into thinking about Kafka's story, the twinges, sensitivities, and aches of the new monstrous form of the very recently former traveling salesman, due to an increasing number of injuries he sustained by attempting to rhythmically rock himself out of bed, move about the room, open his door, and by others, such as the father's kicks, stomps, battery with a cane, and being pummeled with multiple apples, one of which becomes lodged in his shell. At the beginning of the lecture, still feeling hopeful that this was going to be a success, I asked the students to draw what they thought Gregor Samsa looked like, after, or during, his transformation, and then asked for volunteers, who were, as usual, difficult to elicit. One student eventually volunteered, at my grinning supplication, that she thought that Samsa's shell might be hard, and I alighted on this detail, Ah, I said, yes, at the very beginning, he is described as lying on his back as if it was armor, this is the moment of body horror, he was used to sleeping on his right side, but no matter how much he exerted himself he found himself on his back, the multiplicity of his legs waving in the air, a new vibration he was attempting to understand, so surely he had some sort of exoskeleton, but it was vulnerable, as we would see, to abuse. But regardless, this was a trick, asking them to draw Gregor Samsa, as this was meant to be a mystery through the text; Kafka himself insisted that the insect not be drawn on the cover when the novella was published—*Insekt,* he called it, in the German, in a letter to his editor in 1915—although writer and entomologist Vladimir Nabokov, when preparing his own lecture on the story, which he gave in 1953 at Cornell University, where a young Thomas Pynchon was in attendance, drew it anyway, from the front and from the side, and concluded it was obviously a three-foot-long beetle, not a cockroach, as one translation insists, despite being brown, nor a bedbug, the bug here was obviously convex, for one, as shown by how the bedsheets slid off him. I joked to my students, who were completely silent, as they were on mute, that I wished that I had shown up to class wearing a large bug costume, and then not said anything about what I was wearing the entire time, a joke that received a few silent laughs, or at least looks of a congenial pity. The phrase that Kakfa uses, in that malleable opening line, in which Gregor Samsa awakens in his bed and realizes he has transformed, includes two negations—*Ungeheuren Ungeziefer*—that have no literal English translation, as one of his translators, Susan Bernofsky, notes. The loose translation is of an enormous and monstrous unclean verminous thing (*monstrous insect*, she translates), as with Kafka's other animal stories, it's merely suggestive, Bernofsky notes that Kafka intended imprecision, and avoided specificity, in order to have a sense of disorientation for the reader, of blurred perception, just as Gregor Samsa himself experiences, as he comes to, in bed, and begins to understand the changed state in which he's found himself. He's still a person, or he thinks he is, still thinks he's in a dream space, in bed, looking out the window, at the drab weather outside. But he's not a person, he's too overworked, he has worked himself to death, indentured to his hideous parents' debts, and his body refuses to let him move, he transforms himself out of shame. It is a physical pain for him, to stay in bed, and a physicalized sense of dread, of sleeping late, of sleeping past his 4:00 a.m. alarm clock and his train, of missing work and being penalized, it's already 6:00 a.m., and then 7:00 a.m., it's impossible, that this has happened, but also impossible, the idea of getting out of bed, physically impossible, but also the quitting urge is so strong within him that it's become grotesquely somatized. What I didn't tell my students, as I attempted to set the scene for them, to conjure up the room-time of

Gregor Samsa, versus the outside-time, is that day I too attempted to call in sick for this same early evening lecture, although obviously I was not allowed to call in sick, as there I was attempting to deliver it, despite not feeling my best, although it was most likely exhaustion, all I would need, I thought to myself again and again, is a good night's sleep, one night's sleep, to sleep in, maybe one day off, and then I would be fine, ready to face the world again. That day I had written to human resources to ask whether guest faculty were allowed to have sick days. *Guest faculty*, which has been my designation for nearly nine years, even though I am currently teaching a full-time schedule this year at the college, despite not having full-time benefits. I received a rather roundabout email, that she was very sorry to hear how I was feeling, technically guest faculty do accrue sick leave under the state's sick-leave policy, but it's fairly limited, she wrote to me, and used primarily for medical appointments and procedures that are planned in advance. It was difficult for her to comment on the curricular side, whether you can cancel a class without having a substitute arranged, you will have to reach out to your dean for guidance, generally a faculty member will reschedule, but if they absolutely need to, for some unforeseen reason, you do have the option of sick leave, if the class cannot be rescheduled. Like so many bureaucratic communications, the logic was so circular it was difficult to parse actually what was being said. This was the same human resources individual who I had spoken with when at the college and pregnant with my first child, now more than five years ago, who seemed disturbed by my asking whether I was entitled to any leave, since the baby was going to be born toward the end of the semester, and then during a subsequent phone call told me that technically guest faculty did not receive maternity leave. Later my department head told me I could take one or two weeks off "under the table" provided I didn't say anything to human resources, which necessitated that I then begin to avoid her calls asking me when I was due to deliver and whether I knew what I was planning to do. This time around, giving birth during the pandemic, I didn't even tell them that I wanted leave, even though they knew I was pregnant, knowing that this would be met with suspicion, and in fact arranged to be induced one week early, because I was told it would be extremely inconvenient if I were to miss any of the early meetings with students. Because I was teaching over a screen, I was able to hide how sore and uncomfortable I was, bleeding while sitting on the couch, buffeted by pillows, and was able in fact to be seen only as a floating speaking head. I learned I was not supposed to have a body, and for them, I tried not to have one. This was more easily accomplished over the screen, because they could not see my body, or see if it was sore or in pain. With this new technology, I've realized lately, we will never be given an excuse to call in sick again. Even when we are sick, or recovering, we are expected to work, and by *we* I mean those of us who are considered guests and otherwise adjunct, not the tenured faculty who seem to take time off, and frequently cancel classes without making them up, and have maternity leave, and in fact have sabbaticals in which they take semesters or even years off in order to write or not write their books. What was remote were our bodies, our vulnerable health, often related to our precarious status at these institutions, and what the material conditions of our lives were like, all of which we were supposed to hide from view. Obviously I was not able to bring up to the students this communication with human resources or my later correspondence with the dean, that afternoon, but if I had, I daresay it could have contributed to a deeper understanding of Kafka's story of overwork and alienation. I also couldn't point out the weird resonances of the dean, a Nabokov scholar who focused on an ecocritical reading of his work, sprawling lawns of American suburbia, etc., writing me a crisp yet seemingly upbeat letter to the effect that she also didn't know what to tell me, in the academy, she wrote, we did not take "sick days," she made sure to include the quotations, as if it were not an actual phenomenon, it's just not how it works, in the academy, or, for that matter, she wrote, for your purposes, in the creative arts, we have so much flexibility in what we do, she wrote me, that people tend to shift things around. However, she wrote, if it was a case of a colleague having surgery, then no questions asked, we would find a substitute, something to that effect. She wrote me this without having any previous memory of my two pregnancies since she had served as dean, and our communications about it then, and how that courtesy was never extended to me, most likely because she did not consider me a colleague, nor, for that matter, a member of the academy, except for this purpose, that of not having sick leave. I was unsure exactly what she meant about how much flexibility we had, what she meant by both *we* and *flexibility*, as every day, really every hour, was accounted for, with other teaching at other places and work, and the obligations of childcare, for a small child who was home, and another just at kindergarten, and if I had to reschedule, that would just account for more stress, as my summer, which I needed to do other forms of work, such as writing, which was supposed to be my primary profession, and childcare, with both children now home from school, then would get chiseled away. I knew that she was the middle management of higher education that Mark Fisher writes about in *Capitalist Realism*, a pretense of a community that was actually more disciplinary than caring or supportive, and knew that if I pressed on this at all I would just make myself seem somehow suspicious, or lazy, or not someone who was a team player, and so I wrote to her, a single email—"I will work through it!!!"—with triple exclamation points, cheery in the face of her officiousness that masqueraded as camaraderie or, perhaps, wisdom from a mentor. I realized that this meant that the fact of my not feeling well, or feeling rundown, was rendered actually impossible, and perhaps then my pain was just fictional, and I could ignore it, and it would then go away. There was something in the tone of her email, and my immediate response to it, that reminded me of the moment in Kafka's story when the chief clerk comes to the front door at the extremely truant time of 7:00 a.m., an antic hour of silent physical theater having passed, and our stomachs turn, in recognition, at the way his voice goes from cheery to officious to explicitly threatening, while standing outside of Gregor Samsa's bedroom door, in response to what everyone else in that home sees as Gregor Samsa's nonresponse, because it's functionally impossible for him to answer, either because his voice can no longer be detected as human, or because he's afraid of being outed as no longer human, it's difficult to say, he attempted to say something before, and the voice came out squeaking, distorted, and that is part of the drama of the opening first part of the story—how much do the three of the family, standing outside of the door, hear him, or understand him, how much is that even possible? Here, at the incoming presence of the chief clerk, who represents the institutions of capitalism, a father figure even more explicitly villainous than the actual father in the story, the family becomes not animal but servile, as shown through their voices, the mother's and father's overlapping each other, whispering at first, standing outside of their son's door, the clerk approaching, wishing him at first a good morning, cheerily, all of these disembodied voices in syncopation, experienced by Gregor Samsa inside the room, the cheery and officious, the boomingly paternalistic, the high-pitched maternal, the sister's whisper and sob, his own strange and muffled, the parents interjecting with speeches of panic and reassurances, meant for the chief clerk, not for their son. He's not feeling well, the mother says, and the father cuts her off, with a monologue, addressed to father capitalism, all his son does is work, he says to the chief clerk, he lives for his work, he lives and breathes his work, he doesn't go out, he sits at his table and reads his railway timetable or does a little woodwork, his only hobby, he made a picture frame over the last few days, this is the same table in his room that Gregor Samsa regards at the opening, covered with fabric samples, alongside the picture frame on his wall with the woman wearing a fur hat and muff, an advertisement clipped from a magazine, rereading it I am struck by the sensuous textures of this opening, symbolizing his life before, also the melancholy way he now looks out the window, at the drab weather outside, as he does throughout the story, even pushing his armchair over to the window in order to look out, to the leafy street of Charlottenstrasse, the hospital across the way. You must imagine, I did say to my students, speaking through my window, the light changed to darkness outside, the writer, Franz Kafka, performing these voices with their different squeaks and tenors to a laughing group of his friends in his living room, how he would do the voice of the chief clerk, terrifying in his officiousness, in response to the mother pleading that her son just wasn't feeling up to par. "I hope you're right madam," he says, in Michael Hofmann's translation, "I only hope it's nothing serious. Though again I have to say—unhappily or otherwise—we businesspeople often find ourselves in the position of having to set aside some minor ailment, in the greater interest of our work." How the chief clerk pretends to care about Gregor Samsa—but no one cares about Gregor Samsa—and modulates quite quickly from cheery condescension, also terrifying, to a hostile yet paternalistic scold—"Mr. Samsa, what's the matter? You've barricaded yourself into your room, you give us one-word answers, you cause your parents grave and needless anxiety, and—this is just by the by—you're neglecting your official duties in a quite unconscionable way." "You seem set," he says to his employee, quivering behind the door, "on indulging a bizarre array of moods." Perhaps he has missed the train because he has stolen money from the firm, perhaps, and he really hates to say this in front of his parents, but his performance, as of late, has been extremely unsatisfactory, he realizes Christmas is not a good time for sales, but there's never, he says, a good time for no sales. When lying on the couch, preparing for this lecture, I began to wonder again what it would have been like to hear Kafka himself perform these parts, surely he would have gotten the most pleasure squeezing the obnoxiousness from the tonalities of the chief clerk—they exist entirely as disembodied voices, Gregor Samsa's room is a highly attuned earpiece, much like, well, yes, a cockroach, that can hear you coming from another room. At some point I began to switch from reading for the lecture to trying to find a recording of his voice, of which I had heard rumors, first in the first half of a JSTOR article I skimmed through on the squeaking voices of Kafka's animals and their relationship to Blanchot reading Kafka on silence. It appears, at least from the article, that recording devices were sophisticated enough at the time, especially the devices available for Kafka at his workplace, the Workers' Accident Insurance Institute for the Kingdom of Bohemia, for one of his readings to have been recorded, and moreover, his girlfriend, Felice Bauer, worked in the Berlin offices of the Swedish inventor Carl Lindström, where she was supposed to market the parlograph, a dictation machine used in offices to dictate letters. Even though Kafka averred to Felice his phobia for such technology, apparently, for a goof over the Christmas holidays, she was able to smuggle one home for him and his friends, including the Brod brothers, Otto and Max, to play around with, sliding the wax roll into the parlograph in order to make a recording, which then converts the sound vibrations to scratches that could be played back, and he allegedly practiced some of the choral machinations that were in the story he was finishing that December, which gives the opening part of *The Metamorphosis* that desperate energy of a Christmas mood, even though, or even perhaps because, he didn't celebrate the holiday. There is a compressed file that I found on a deep subreddit on everything about the Prague author, r/stainlessquiet, that professes to be a scratchy minute of reading which I clicked on and listened to—I cannot understand German, although, I believe, I know when that is the language being spoken. I'm not sure exactly what I was listening to, it didn't appear to be German, but a series of squeaks followed by silences and then irrepressible laughter. I was unsure whether this apparently found recording was a hoax, or if this was how Kafka interpreted the noises that poor Gregor Samsa emitted when in a panic, realizing he was in danger of disciplinary action, and violently hurrying out of bed, but not realizing that his new body wasn't the same instrument he had used to produce human voices, the perversity of his horrible sounds being that he loved and craved music, specifically his sister Grete's violin, which stirs him to the point of exposure, he cannot even bear it, and finally, to real banishment and death, one March evening, the same time of year that it was now, as I was preparing for and then giving this lecture. But it is left up to interpretation, when Gregor Samsa answers "no" to his father asking if they can open the door to the chief clerk, punctuated by his sister's sobs behind the door on the other side, whether the humans listening to him can hear that "no" or heard something like an awful silence. The chief clerk states in the escalating monologue that follows that his errant employee is only giving one-word answers, so apparently that "no" was transmitted, but more like the scratching sound that appears on the recording, perhaps that was the author's, or some copycat's, painful yet hilarious interpretation, a "no" that felt like a cockroach's chirp or hiss, although it would then matter whether Kafka felt that Gregor Samsa was actually speaking words, but that his functions had deteriorated, the question being how close his animal voices are to his voice. I wished when I was transmitting my Zoom lecture to bored or expectant faces, when their faces were shown to me, I could communicate to them how my own tone changed over email, at the implicit and passive assertions of my dean, how it took on a different vibration at this nonrecognition, became cheery in my desperation, meant to make clear how punctual I will always be, what a good worker I was, although I never would have communicated this to them, out of shame as to what I could turn into, out of my constant fear of precarity, assuring the dean that *I will work through it!!!* followed by three unctuous exclamation points, as if to underscore that ha ha ha, no biggie, after all, I understood that—unhappily or otherwise—we in the academy, for I was certainly as well a member, however untenured, sometimes have to work through such minor ailments for the overall good of The Work. When I hit reply, I received a vacation email that her break had just started, as it was spring break for the college beginning that Friday. The stress at even the prospect of losing this position vibrated throughout my body, the absurdity of my current condition, that I need to teach to pay for the studio that we rent for an outlandish price out back, that previously stored our landlord's carpentry equipment, the idea was that I would use this space, more like a dark cave, in order to write, but I don't have time to write, all I do is go inside, switch on the light, and teach, to mostly darkened screens with their video cameras turned off, so that often I felt like I was speaking to myself alone within a shadowy room. Maybe it made sense that their middle-aged professor, who was often sweating, unprepared, and seemed glazed with exhaustion, would identify more with Gregor Samsa's struggles than their own, maybe they were only a couple years away from feeling trapped within capitalism, and could pretend that this would not be their future, or maybe they were privileged to know that there wasn't an imminent need to support a family based on their income, which could go away at any second. I began performing, as I tended to do over Zoom, in an attempt to elicit their attention, Kafka's obsequious monologue, his panic-attack protestations, we can imagine a chattering, even high-pitched tone correct and servile like out of a story by Robert Walser. You must understand, I said to them, the effect of the chief clerk's presence on his nervous system, the fight and flight response catalyzed by his increasingly unsubtle threats, an extreme excitement that causes him to ricochet himself out of bed and begin to plead to this middle manager with a monologue of invocations and apologies. I tried to sound out for them the rhythms of this interlude, the awful, totalizing silence that results after Gregor Samsa attempts to speak, that makes it clear that he cannot be understood, that he has become increasingly incomprehensible. "'That was the voice of an animal,' said the chief clerk, strikingly much more quiet than his mother's screaming." The commotion that results, Gregor Samsa damaging his body with his exertions attempting to unlock the door with his newly powerful mandibles, almost losing consciousness attempting to turn the key, the brown liquid dribbling out of him, the stickiness of this language, the commotion, the convulsion at this monstrous sighting, something like slapstick or farce if it wasn't so terrible. The sad sight of the son, always away traveling, finally seeing the bright light of the day, the father at leisure eating breakfast and perusing newspapers for hours, sputtering out a lengthy monologue of work-ese, speaking corporate language, already absurd, that Kafka renders more absurd with an unrecognizable squeak, I am unsure but I believe this is the section being performed in the recording, something about the frantic pace of the voice speaking, that sounds like a creature scratching or hissing, it's impossible to decipher, except something of the frequency. But just as I'm acting out, in my way, the different voices in this family tragedy as well as farce, I realize, suddenly, that my students haven't been able to hear anything I've said, possibly since the chief clerk's entrance, possibly even earlier, and that the sound has gone in and out of the lecture. Can anyone hear me, I said, and when they didn't respond, I began to slightly panic, and I began to stare at all of their faces, realizing I was unable to tell, in general, whether they were frozen or whether they were just not responding at all, thinking perhaps I could see one student blink, but I couldn't be certain. Finally, someone in the chat let me know they could now hear me, in and out, but they couldn't see me, a predicament, I realized, which seemed to be reenacting what happens in part one of *The Metamorphosis*, Gregor Samsa not knowing whether he is being comprehended, and often met with silence, or nonresponse, and then later, the absence of any direct human address at all. I began the lecture again, and it seemed, at least, that it was working, until they froze again, or I froze, and this became the unrelenting rhythm of a tortured monologue, which again, I later thought, mirrored Kafka's story, perhaps the only way to give a lecture on it was to deliver it completely mute, or with my face distorted, unrecognizable. I was sitting there, in a room gone completely dark except for my square of bright artificial light, increasingly paranoid that no one could hear me at all, and receiving almost no reassurances from the students, as I began to try to lead them into the second part, what Nabokov calls the drama of duration, in which Gregor Samsa increasingly loses his memories of the outside world, his appetite as well as his vision, finding in the window that he still sits at a view that is becoming dark and blurry; my computer kept telling me that my connection was unstable. At some point, I kept on being kicked out of the room, and, stressed out, sweating, like the man running from the room that was the first cover illustration used for *The Metamorphosis*. I ran with my laptop back into my apartment, and into my bedroom, and, on my unmade bed, shadowy in the screen, I attempted to move through the disintegration, his monotonous life, his desire to have his room emptied out of furniture like a cave, so close to forgetting his human life he stops eating, a hunger artist, he desires to disappear, to spare his family more suffering. Finally it is the end of March, as it was now, he is finally dead, he is not Gregor Samsa anymore, he is not their son or brother, he is a thing to be disposed of, by the charwoman, while the family takes the tram to a park, to enjoy the spring day. I perform the demise of Gregor Samsa, while the screen freezes and flickers, while my voice becomes a weird tinny thing, garbled and unrecognizable, Did you get any of that? I said mournfully at the end, all of the screens almost dark, but it sputtered out again, before any of them could say, or maybe they just didn't say anything at all, or maybe I was unable to comprehend their voices.

MY KAFKA SYSTEM (BRIEF OBSERVATIONS OF THE EUROPEAN MALE)

ON NAKEDNESS PART ONE

The Müller system, as proselytized by the Danish gymnast Jørgen Peter Müller in his bestselling 1904 pamphlet of exercises, *My System*, instructed practitioners to exercise in their underwear, ideally in the open air, for fifteen minutes a day. The cover featured the Greek athlete Apoxyomenos in statuary. A contemporary photograph of Müller himself accentuates his muscular physique, posed like a circus acrobat, adorned only with a twirly mustache and tighty-whities. *My System* was targeted to gentlemen dandies who spent all day in a café, like our Kafka. The system prescribed an ordered series of elaborate stretches, hops, windmills, lunges. Kafka followed the system religiously, always a ready convert to any cult of natural eating or physical fitness. I can imagine his stick-thin frame, with cartoonishly baggy white underwear, standing in front of his open window. To imagine Kafka as a naked body is to imagine him as an animal. John Berger: "To be naked is to be oneself." I like to think of this series that follows as *My Kafka System*.

ON JOSEPH PILATES

In his German circus troupe, he played the Greek statue. Above the long slender bodies of dancers, Katherine Hepburn, he stood, tanned and muscled bare chest, in his tight shorts and espadrilles, so certain. Cigar in his mouth, the whiskey, the glass eye. His wife, Clara, severe in a matron's uniform. At first his regime fixated on the masculine physique, but the women felt worse about themselves and kept on returning. Kafka would have been an ideal consumer—he always felt wretched about himself. Touring England in 1914, Pilates became a prisoner on the Isle of Man. He was amazed at his fellows' somnolence. You men with your gray faces! He shouted at them. Why can't you look like animals?

Look at a cat! He outfitted hospital beds with pulleys and devices, for bodies to strain and stretch like cats. The men felt better, after the war, then before. After thirty sessions, Joseph Pilates would say, you would have an entirely new body. But if one had an entirely new body, how could one be sure it was still one's body at all? This question of the *I* and its arduous, even torturous, relationship to the mortal body seems inherently a question for Franz Kafka. In 1914 Kafka had already begun his story of an island penal colony, and the complex machine that inscribed the prison sentence on the inmate's skin.

ON RUDOLF STEINER

In March 1911, the spring before leaving on his second European tour, Kafka attended several lectures on theosophy by Rudolf Steiner, including one on "occult physiology," with a focus on the spiritual forces that can be reawakened through the body, its organs, etc. ("Man's Inner Cosmic System," "The Blood as Manifestation and Instrument of the Human Ego"). This was exactly Kafka's sort of thing. Of course, in a state of crisis in regards to his day life of work vs. his nocturnal writing existence, he wanted to know what this meant, to both fortify the mystical experiences of the I, or ego, as well as desire to escape it, in terms of his writing. He visited Steiner at the Hotel Victoria, on Jungmannstrasse, and poured out all of his feelings regarding his happiness as it related to his writing, his misery as it related to his writing. He writes a journal entry about this visit, recording what he confessed to Steiner. Perhaps, Herr Doktor, I have come close to this clairvoyance you describe, I have come close to the limits of both the self and the human, but if I convert entirely . . . Rudolf Steiner apparently was silent for most of the monologue. Finally, he said, "Mr. Kafka, don't eat eggs."

ON BUTCHERS

Obviously this has to do with his father, also built like a boxer, twirly mustache, brimming with vitality. The grotesque way, in his 1919 forty-five-page revenge letter, Kafka remembers witnessing, as a child, his father's vigorous appetite and messy eating, cracking bones with his teeth, cleaning and cutting his fingernails at the table. Kafka's strict vegetarian diet certainly seems to be a reaction to witnessing his father's bullying and strenuous eating at the table, as well as his revulsion to the horrors of his paternal grandfather, who was a butcher (as was mine, incidentally). In "The Lives of Animals," part of Coetzee's series of fictional lectures given by his alter ego, Elizabeth Costello, there is a scene of the grandchildren eating separately, as they're having chicken for dinner, as the elderly novelist, who has lectured on Kafka and animal rights over a year, refuses to be around meat, much to the scorn of the daughter-in-law, who is an out-of-work moral philosopher. Elizabeth Costello focuses her traveling lectures on the horror of the lives of animals, including connecting factory farming to the Holocaust, and the metaphor, as has often been employed when thinking of Kafka's animal stories, of Jews killed in the camps being treated like animals (sheep to the slaughter, Nazi butchers, etc.). Kafka often depicted himself as a slaughtered animal in his letters and notebooks, his body cut up by a butcher's knife. "Jackals and Arabs," his 1917 short story, is often read as a parable of the Jew, of kosher slaughter, especially because it was published, along with "A Report to an Academy," in the magazine *Der Jude* ("the Jew") by Martin Buber. But perhaps it's actually, like other of Kafka's stories, about his identification with the nonhuman, reinforced by his vegetarianism. Don't call them parables, he told Martin Buber. If anything, call them animal stories.

ON ZOO STORIES

Upon going to an aquarium in Berlin, walking along the illuminated tanks, Kafka reportedly began to speak to the fish swimming by: "Now at last I can look at you in peace, I don't eat you anymore."

ON METAPHORS AND PARABLES

In a journal entry in 1921, Kafka wrote, "Metaphors are one of the things that make me despair of literature." This is quoted by Deleuze and Guattari in their 1975 essay on Kafka, "What Is a Minor Literature?" They write, "Metamorphosis is the contrary of metaphor." It can't be a parable, exactly (theological, psychoanalytic, existential alienation), if there is no lesson to the parable, no easy reading. Walter Benjamin, in his essay on the tenth anniversary of Kafka's death, writes: "his parables are never exhausted by what is explainable; on the contrary, he took all conceivable precautions against the interpretation of his writings."

ON FASTING

In Kafka's stories, fasting sharpens the senses, leads to a metamorphosis, a separation from the human, into the nonhuman, then death, which is the opposite of metamorphosis. In "Investigations of a Dog," the speaker begins a quasi-scientific inquiry regarding where food comes from, if it comes from the earth, and, like Gregor Samsa in *The Metamorphosis*, avers that he was force fed, feasts upon music. Gregor Samsa, having found himself now nonhuman, finds his appetite completely changed—only wanting rotting food, not fresh, sucking on cheese, on bones congealed in white sauce. It's butchers who watch "Ein Hungerkünstler" to make sure he doesn't eat secretly, but then he's forgotten and disappears into the corner of his cage. The panther that replaces him in the cage eats raw meat, refreshed, struts powerfully around (because he's not fasting). The creature in "The Burrow" is *not* a rat, dear D & G, but it does sometimes find itself in a somnolent stupor, the tail of a rat between his teeth, eating little creatures along the way (becoming-molecular after becoming-animal, I guess). The kitten-lamb hybrid in another Kafka animal story is fasting by default—it can only survive on milk (Gregor Samsa's first dish, brought out prettily to his room by Grete with pieces of bread), because his lamb half won't eat meat and his cat-half won't eat grass.

ON HYBRIDITY

When anyone brings up "hybrid writing," in the future, I want to point to Kafka's story "A Crossbreed," brief observations of a cat-lamb who also wants to be a dog. It is one of Kafka's only stories about a pet (besides "Blumfeld, an Elderly Bachelor," about tiny bouncing balls who become creaturely, in a way, more of his obsession with smallness). The way a pet completes a human, John Berger writes sardonically of this codependence in "Why Look at Animals?" The pet is a mirror for its person. But one does not really see the other. Kafka is perhaps ironically sending this up—when the creature is on the speaker's lap, he looks and sees tears falling from its whiskers—but whose tears were they? There is no reciprocal recognition among animals in the story—just as Berger predicted. Donna Haraway, in her notion of companion species, finds something much more beautiful about this merging, this identification, the self and the nonself, the human and the nonhuman (the "humanimal," she calls it, in a YouTube mini lecture, bridging her hands together in a gesture).

ON DONALD DUCK

How alienated from the animal we are, writes John Berger, in his takedown of the Victorian zoo. Take pets and the ways that humans have become codependent with them, seeing themselves through them, the ways they have grown to resemble each other. (Children are, briefly, somewhat different, he adds, parenthetically. What does this mean? That children are different from pets? That children regard pets somewhat differently?) The disgust he feels for the petty dialogues between Donald Duck and his nephews, the gross capitalist narrative. Remember, writing his treatise on watching animals, on the miseries of their captivity, in 1977, the fifty-year-old critic is newly again a father, this time of a one-year-old. His other children grown. Now imagine (briefly) him cranky again at the zoo, cranky watching Disney cartoons, cranky reading Beatrix Potter.

ON ANIMALS IMAGINED BY KAFKA

A fragment reproduced in Borges's bestiary, *The Book of Imaginary Beings*:

> It is the animal with the big tail, a tail many yards long and like a fox's brush. How I should like to get my hands on this tail sometime, but it is impossible, the animal is constantly moving about, the tail is constantly being flung this way, and that. The animal resembles a kangaroo, but not as to the face. . . . Sometimes I have the feeling that the animal is trying to tame me.

The strange old man with wings in the second octavo notebook feels like a sketch for the Gabriel García Márquez story "A Very Old Man with Enormous Wings," which also has "A Hunger Artist" freak show vibes (as well as the competing carnival attraction of a woman changed into a spider for disobeying her parents!). In Kafka's fragment, unlike García Márquez's, the wings do not work.

• • •

ON THE HUMAN ZOO

It seems likely that Kafka did attend a so-called human zoo exhibit, at the Hagenbeck Zoo in Prague. These regular exhibits at European and American zoos and circuses, products of Victorian scientific racism and colonial curiosity, featured unpaid, often indigenous non-European performers, dressed nearly naked in animal skins. Often they were not prepared for the cold, as in the García Márquez story, and also died of preventable illnesses, such as smallpox. There is the story of one Ota Benga, a Congolese man purchased by slave traders and exhibited in the Bronx Zoo, amidst the orangutans. An Inuit man, Abraham Ulrikab, wrote a diary of his experiences living in a human zoo, including in Prague, around the year Kafka was born. His reports are eerily similar to "A Hunger Artist"—the guards outside the cages all day and night.

ON KAFKA'S IDENTIFICATION WITH THE NONHUMAN

"Often—and in my inmost self perhaps all the time—I doubt whether I am a human being," he wrote to Felice. He repeats this later in the letter: "I am not a human being." An aphorism, from the time he spent at his sister's farm in Zürau: "To animalize is human, to humanize is animal." It is the human who have created the category of animal, writes Jacques Derrida.

ON NAKEDNESS PART TWO

When the philosopher emerged from the shower, he found himself unable to meet the gaze of his cat, feeling suddenly ashamed of his nakedness. It was a limit-experience with the nonhuman, akin to the bourgeois sculptor G. H. trancing out after ingesting a cockroach in Clarice Lispector's novel. Shame is the strongest gesture of Kafka, writes Walter Benjamin. Curious to think of shame as a gesture—is it done with hands, arms, covering the body? (Animals in Kafka's stories suddenly have arms or hands when they shouldn't, suggestive of a hybrid species.) This encounter with Jacques Derrida's own nakedness, and realizing his animal is not naked, because they're already naked, catalyzed a series of lectures (an hour a day, over ten days) at a conference devoted to his thinking entitled "The Autobiographical Animal."

It's in this series of lectures that Derrida makes a gesture to "Kafka's vast zoopoetics," triggering an entire field of criticism. Donna Haraway thinks that Derrida misses a chance at meditating upon the meeting of species, in his encounter with his cat encountering him: it's all his shame, his ego, his cogito. "Incurious, he missed a possible invitation, a possible introduction to other-worlding."

ON OTTLA'S CAT

The most time Kafka spent among actual animals was at his sister Ottla's farm in Zürau in the summer of 1917, convalescing from his first flare-up of tuberculosis. He would stay there almost a year, observing the pigs, feeding the goats in the garden. His closest companion was Ottla's cat, who surprised him by jumping on his lap. Although he didn't like it when he had to undress in front of the cat, for his daily exercises. Like Jacques Derrida eighty years later, he found it unnerving. She often stayed in the empty room next to his, so she wouldn't dirty his room, her excretions all over the sofa and rug. Their proximity was necessary, as she caught the mice for him that also unnerved him. More on that later.

ON THE AUTOBIOGRAPHICAL ANIMAL

In the first part of Yoko Tawada's generational triptych *Memoirs of a Polar Bear*, the Russian retired circus performer, the grandmother to the celebrity zoo polar bear Knut, is emigrated to Germany and compelled to write her life story, for payment in chocolate and salmon. She visits a bookstore and is lectured by Friedrich the clerk on the animal stories of Kafka. Why, she wonders, does she have to be an autobiographical animal, unlike the animal narrators, if that's the best word for them, or speakers (squeakers?) who are allowed to live in the present tense, and don't have to dig up all the trauma of childhood? "Something that can disappear is called 'I,'" she internally observes. Yes, these aren't memoirs, they are more like reports or investigations. Although there is that moment in "Investigations of a Dog" where the lead canine investigator (is this what I'm calling a narrator?) circles around a childhood memory of being a young pup, watching dogs perform in a pyramid, a blurry circus memory. Which makes me wonder, is Kafka an autobiographical animal? His letters and diaries certainly have the memoir impulse Derrida wonders about, the I-impulse. Do his animal stories?

ON BEEKEEPING

The grandmother polar bear is an institutionalized animal, constantly attending lectures, panels, conferences, including on "The Future of Beekeeping." This reminds me again of Rudolf Steiner, who I think about a lot more than I'd like to admit, including braving a rickety ladder up to the rooftop of my children's school to look at the colonies of bees. His nine lectures on bees, given to workmen at the Goetheanum in Dornach, Switzerland, in 1923 (the year before Kafka's death, the fertile period of his major late animal stories), have some of the quasi-scientific but also metaphysical vibes, if you can call them that, of Kafka's parafictional lectures. That's the strange thing about a lecture presented as a story, as Elizabeth Costello notes of "A Report to an Academy," a meta nod to what we are reading—we don't actually know who is speaking, and who the audience is. All we have is the text of the lecture. The lecture hall, she notes, could actually be a zoo.

• • •

ON MIMICRY

The obsequiousness with which the speaker apes his report feels decidedly inspired by Rudolf Steiner and other quasi-scentific lectures Kafka must have attended. The formality of the address, "Esteemed Gentleman of the Academy! You show me the honor of calling upon me to submit a report concerning my previous life as an ape." It was not freedom the hostage, once captured by bounty hunters, looked for, there was no real freedom, but a way out. Homi Bhabha borrows the term "mimicry" from Lacan, who got it from zoology. The postcolonial aping required to stand in the margins of the dominant class. Through language, primarily. When she is giving her lecture, Elizabeth Costello says she feels like Red Peter when she gave her previous lecture, but here is where Coetzee's argument feels a bit sketchy. Is she Red Peter because she's a woman, camouflaging herself by speaking of Kafka, and no one is interested in a woman speaking of Kafka? The woman writer is supposed to be the real autobiographical animal. Her childhood, etc. "But audiences don't react well to heavy historical self-ironization. They might at a pinch accept it from a man, but not from a woman.

A woman doesn't need to wear all that armor." That is from a woman critic, who later, inevitably, beds Elizabeth Costello's son, who is always the main character in the oedipal duo of mother and son, the esteemed author split in two. Women are good at mimicry, the journalist says. But can't his mother write a dog? The son argues. Can't a man write a woman? That seems to be a side argument of what Coetzee is interrogating, in the "What Is Realism?" of the title. But also: when Kafka writes about an ape he is talking about an ape. It is, cautiously, true that the first person in a lecture or report can also obscure gender, as well as other considerations, like species.

ON SULTAN'S BANANA

When speaking on "A Report to an Academy," Elizabeth Costello traces what she thinks might be the real-life inspiration for Red Peter—Sultan the chimpanzee, studied (and tested) in a series of cognitive experiments by gestalt psychologist Wolfgang Köhler on the island of Tenerife. She theorizes that Kafka would be aware of Köhler's research, as he was also interested in Darwin (although here, metamorphosis is the opposite of extinction). It's not that

Sultan was trained to think, it's that he was trained to get the banana, by stacking the boxes. We do know that Kafka drew on the experiments of the thinking horses of Elberfeld for his story "A Young and Ambitious Student," satirizing the repetition of these experiments to test whether Clever Hans the horse was trained by Wilhelm von Osten to recognize unconscious signaling or whether he was an equine mathematical genius.

ON INVESTIGATIONS OR REPORTS

As has been well traced, Kafka was an investigator for the Workers' Accident Insurance Institute, and the other writing he did was in the form of accidental reports with a specific technical tone. He often uses this language of the investigation, as well as the written report, for his animal stories, like a personal favorite, the unfinished "The Village Schoolmaster," written in the winter of 1914 to 1915 and subsequently abandoned, as happens often with the animal stories, because otherwise they would never end. This is distinct from a report as issued by an insurance investigator that by its nature has to be finite, for the case to be closed. In Kafka's investigations, sometimes observing an animal or from the perspective of a humanimal, there is often a riddle as to what is even being investigated. "The Village Schoolmaster," in a translation by Michael Hofmann, bears parallels to what I might call the triptych of late animal stories, marked by their digressiveness and disorientation. The narrator remembers the story of a giant mole that brought brief fame to a small village, as documented in a pamphlet written by a local schoolmaster. The story is narrated by a writer, somewhat in the mode of Borges's Pierre Menard, who wants to think through and rewrite the report, carrying out all of his investigations in a parallel way, causing antagonism between the original author and the follow-up investigator. The narrator, like in many of the animal stories, is one of what Benjamin, probably thinking through Robert Walser, calls one of Kafka's assistants. And because of this, there is always at first a flattering or complimentary nature to the description of the first author, which then becomes murky in hostility and ambivalence. "It was really as though no one had investigated the case at all, as though I were the first to interview the witnesses, the first to collate the accounts, the first to draw conclusions." His follow-up paper, like the originary pamphlet, is of course a failure, and not only that, most readers confused them with each other. Like the other late animal stories, it is quite possible to read this, and the other reports, as Kafka's meditations on his own writing, his other, subterranean, nocturnal work.

ON MARKING TERRITORY

Now I'm worried, as we move toward the end, toward these last animal stories, we are also going overlong. The report becomes absurd, mired in a sort of riddle or metaphysical maze. The animal investigators are almost always nocturnal, much like the atmosphere in which Kafka wrote them, most likely on a sickbed, even deathbed, if it's an interminably long one, even if the animal is not a creature of the night (is a dog, for example, but then there are the mice and the mole-like last creature). There's an almost insomniac quality to the questioning of the solitary canine investigator, self-excluded and alienated from his pack, aware of his own mortality. There is the I but also, so often, a longing for a *we*, what D & G call the "collective utterances." I'm going to now repeat this in a different way, it feels important. Of Kafka's animal stories, "There is no subject, there are only collective arrangements of utterance." No stable subject, but a multiplicity. The narrator is unreliable. Also porous. As always ambivalence toward others in the species/family/collectivity enters. A dog marks territory, says D & G. Hence: language in the animal stories is (this is so Deleuzian) "deterritorialized."

ON WHISTLING

There is a whistling sound throughout the last late triptych of animal stories (late, later, he died at forty, he was dying of tuberculosis for seven years, this is the other atmosphere of the fiction, mortality, the absurdity and failure of the body, the way time is interminable, ongoing, during illness). The musicality specific to the dog species in the previous story. There is the "whistling" sound that the creature in "The Burrow" observes, paranoidly, not knowing where it's coming from, interior or exterior (as critics have noted, Kafka also referred to his wheezing cough as "his animal"). And of course, there's Josephine the Singer—how to characterize her voice, a supernumerary member of the community theorizes, changing his tune or tone throughout this delightfully, absurdly boring story. Perhaps it's just what our people do, he thinks—perhaps it's just whistling.

ON VOICE

Is it even art? That is the main, infuriating, constantly in flux series of questions in "Josephine the Singer, or the Mouse People." As has been noted, the only real mention of a mouse is in the title, besides a mention of fur, but that's enough (it's a trick, a sort of theater, we find ourselves in the auditorium, witnessing the otherwise mute Josephine perform sublime miracles). Kafka's animal lectures are the opposite of silence but often about silence—there's no dialogue in them, although Josephine's dialogue is often imagined by the anonymous mouse-laborer who both worships the chanteuse and finds her a complete fraud, a tension between the individual and her community, his feelings about art incredibly ambivalent (as always, there are many interpretations that the story is about Jewish music, or about the Jews as mouse people, etc.). Long, winding sentences, like a running of the mouth, repetitive, so much of the language getting lost, dissolving. Like so much theater, it can be a performance of endurance. This or "The Burrow" are the last two stories Kafka wrote, in the winter of 1923 to 1924, before he died that June.

ON MICE

It's not a surprise, perhaps, that these two last stories deal with the persistence of burrowing creatures. The horror of Kafka's life in Zürau were the mice hordes who kept him up at night with their noise—their crawling and gnawing in the walls. The phobia was also a fear of tiny creatures, of creatures living in the walls who were nocturnal like him, a competition for the desired silence he needed in order to be alive, or a writer. The mice infestation ran through all of his letters from that period. His rants sound like something out of "The Burrow." (Panic and dread have such a fast energy in the story, and his letters, the words running around like tiny, silent animals digging through the walls!) But Ottla's cat helped, also, later, traps were set. The creature in "The Burrow" is not a mouse, it's maybe more like a mole, it's purposefully blurry, like Gregor Samsa, the first animal story.

ON THE PRESENT TENSE

This is the most maddening, interminable text you'll ever read. One doesn't read "The Burrow" as much as tunnel through it, the passages are long and unbroken, there are, Coetzee observes in what might have been his dissertation, no breaks in narration or breaks in thirty-five pages of text (one break for sleep, he notes). Time in the burrow is durational, yet complex and baffling, the more he reads the text. Animals live in an ongoing present tense, the setting, possibly the subject, of this story. "The present here is an iterative, habitual present, with a cycle of seasons and even years." The real subject of the burrow is the labyrinth itself, and one's entire life organized around it, becoming it, the interior becomes the exterior, the burrow itself a body, the I becoming a *we* (subject of Kafka's stories). "I and the burrow belong so indissolubly together." It is the monologue of a creature entirely alone. The story is unfinished, like many of Kafka's stories. Deleuze and Guattari have a theory about why only the stories are about animals and the novels aren't about termites, for instance. In a Kafka story it ends when the creature finds a way out—or just is unfinished if there's an impasse. The ending of the last story seems correct however, for a story about the ongoingness of a project where the only escape or ending is death "but everything went on unchanged—"

ACKNOWLEDGMENTS

Grateful acknowledgment to the editors of the journals in which the following reports and lectures have appeared, sometimes in slightly different form: *VQR*: "The Missing Person" and "Monkey House"; *The Yale Review*: "The Winter Zoo"; *The White Review*: "*Insekt* or large verminous thing"; *BOMB*: "On Donald Duck"; *Cost of Paper*: "On Joseph Pilates."

Gratitude as well to the students in the yearlong, remote literature lecture on The Animal I taught at Sarah Lawrence College from fall 2021 to spring 2022, when I had a one-year-old baby at home. Also I am thinking of Bhanu Kapil appearing over Zoom with me and Una Chung for a guest lecture on The Animal, and how catalyzing that experience felt for me.

Thanks to Transit Books, for publishing this strange study in their Undelivered Lectures series.

Thanks as well to friends who have read these reports and encouraged me to write more, especially Sofia Samatar.

Love to my zoo companions, who saw this world with me and often reported back—John, Leo, and Rainer.

KATE ZAMBRENO is the author, most recently, of *Drifts*; *To Write As If Already Dead*, a study of Hervé Guibert; *The Light Room*; and a collaborative study on tone in literature with Sofia Samatar. They live in Brooklyn with their two children and their partner, John Vincler. A 2021 Guggenheim Fellow in Nonfiction, they are a PhD candidate in performance studies at NYU.